Educational Attainments

Issues and Outcomes
in Multicultural Education

Educational Attainments

Issues and Outcomes
in Multicultural Education

Edited by

Gajendra Verma

and

Peter Pumfrey

 The Falmer Press

(A member of the Taylor & Francis Group)
London • New York • Philadelphia

UK	The Falmer Press, Falmer House, Barcombe, Lewes, East Sussex, BN8 5DL
USA	The Falmer Press, Taylor & Francis Inc., 242 Cherry Street, Philadelphia, PA 19106-1906

First published 1988

Library of Congress Cataloguing in Publication Data

Educational attainments: issues and outcomes in multicultural education/
edited by Gajendra Verma and Peter Pumfrey. p. cm.
    Papers from four symposia, two which were sponsored by the
Committee of the Division of Educational and Child Psychology of
the British Psychological Society, one sponsored by the International
Centre for Intercultural Studies of the University of Bradford, and the
other sponsored by the Centre for Educational Guidance and Special
Needs of the University of Manchester.
    Bibliography: p.
    Includes index.
    ISBN 1-85000-308-4   ISBN 1-85000-309-2 (pbk.)
    1. Minorities — Education — Great Britain.   2. Intercultural educa-
tion — Great Britain.   3. Pluralism (Social sciences) — Great Britain.
4. Academic achievement. I. Verma, Gajendra K. II. Pumfrey,
Peter. III. British Psychological Society. Division of Educational and
Child Psychology. Committee. IV. University of Bradford. International Centre for Intercultural Studies.   V. University of Manchester. Centre for Educational Guidance and Special Needs.

LC3736.G6E336 1988	87-35991
370.19′34′0941 — dc 19	CIP

Jacket design by Caroline Archer

Typeset in 11/13 Bembo by
Imago Publishing Ltd, Thame, Oxon.

*Printed in Great Britain by
Redwood Burn Limited, Trowbridge, Wiltshire
and bound by Pegasus Bookbinding, Melksham, Wiltshire*

Contents

Contents

Acknowledgements

The chapters comprising this book derive from presentations made at four recent symposia, organized by the editors, devoted to the topic.

We gratefully acknowledge the support of professional organizations, individuals and educational institutions in producing this book. The Committee of the Division of Educational and Child Psychology of the British Psychological Society sponsored two international symposia bearing on the matters with which this book is concerned and also gave their permission for the use of certain papers that were presented. Additionally, we are indebted to individuals who contributed to a symposium organized under the aegis of the former International Centre for Intercultural Studies of the University of Bradford. Finally, our thanks are due to the Centre for Ethnic Studies in Education and the Centre for Educational Guidance and Special Needs of the University of Manchester for encouraging the editors to mount a national conference on multicultural education in October 1986.

Individuals from different ethnic groups and from different professional orientations have contributed to this book. The editors consider that this heterogeneity has added considerably to its value. In their different ways all the chapters contribute to conceptualizing, analyzing and describing issues and outcomes related to enhancing the educational attainments of all our pupils. That is the valid concern of multicultural education. The demanding and arduous secretarial tasks involved in preparing the manuscript were efficiently carried out by Annette McKie and Kay Poisner. To them we extend our sincere thanks. The editors, however, bear full responsibility for the final product.

Gajendra K. Verma
Peter P. Pumfrey

Introduction

Gajendra Verma and Peter Pumfrey

This collection of chapters on the broad theme of educational attainment in a multicultural setting aims to review recent thinking and research in the fields of education, ethnicity and cross-cultural processes. It brings together chapters using a variety of methodological approaches. The chapters in this volume have been given at recent related conferences, but none has been published in its present form. The contributors to this book have reported research which indicate strategies for rethinking, action or change in the field of education in a plural society. The issues dealt with are contemporary, complex and controversial. They are also of considerable importance. They bear on the opportunities accorded to all pupils attending British educational institutions, to those who provide education and to the society within which education in embedded.

Multicultural education is a system of education which, in an ethnically complex society, attempts to meet the cultural, cognitive and self concept needs of groups and individuals from diverse ethnic backgrounds. In addition, such education aims to promote equality of educational achievement between groups, mutuality of respect and tolerance. The ultimate aim is equality of status, resource access and economic power between different ethnic groups within British society. Thus, the focus in educational provision initially moved towards the design of programmes intended to promote unity whilst allowing for diversity. Such programmes sought to meet the 'special needs' of ethnic minority children in the British educational system.

In the two decades following the end of World War II, increasing numbers of immigrants from former British colonies (for example, the Caribbean, the Indian subcontinent, East Africa) came to the United Kingdom. At that time it was generally assumed that providing support during the initial period of adjustment would lead to the *assimilation* of the immigrant groups into the host community, just as it was thought that previous groups of immigrants had been absorbed. This phase was one that caused minimal disturbance to the indigenous majority as the emphasis was on educational programmes for the acquisition of English by non-English-speaking children (particularly Asians). A change gradually took place during the 1960s when knowledge of the respective cultures from which the immigrants came was increasingly seen as important to their education in the UK. Assimilation evolved into an implicit policy aiming at *integration*. As British-born children of parents of minority ethnic groups, the second generation ·of ethnic minority pupils, began to work their ways through the educational system, it was realized that neither assimilation nor integration had been realised. The importance of *cultural pluralism*, the valuing of the distinctive contributions of the diversity of ethnic groups in the UK, began to be seen as one way of building on what had been learned from the previous two phases.

Pluralism involves different cultural and ethnic groups in the same society not merely existing side by side, but understanding sympathetically each other's folklore, lifestyles, literature, customs and aspirations. The pluralist approach consists of two essential complementary elements: (a) equality of opportunity relating to educational, social and political issues; and (b) retention and maintenance of ethnic identity and distinct culture. Multicultural and antiracist education are developing as aspects of cultural pluralism.

Britain is a multicultural, multiethnic society. It contains very many British children who can also be described as members of minority ethnic groups. A substantial proportion of these can be distinguished from the majority ethnic groups on the basis of skin colour. Many of the minority ethnic groups can be characterized by particular sets of religious and cultural values. They are, in many instances, also identifiable by income (low), housing (poor) and other indices of material deprivation. Thus, inequalities relating to ethnic origin can be found in many features of day-to-day life.

In any industrialized society one of the major avenues to career opportunities is through achieving relative success in the educational system. Competence in the basic fields of literacy and numeracy are valued both for the opportunities they open up and the power that they give to individuals to understand, enrich and control their lives. Unemployment and education are inextricably linked; employability depends to a large extent on educational success. At the same time it must be recognized that young people of Afro-Caribbean and Asian descent who are seeking jobs are not treated in the same way as those from the majority group who have similar qualifications.

The purpose of this book is to present a contemporary account of some of the key issues involved in multicultural education together with recent evidence concerning the educational attainments of pupils drawn from certain minority ethnic groups. We have concentrated on British Afro-Caribbean and British Asians, since these are by far the biggest groups and the ones that have been the main focus of most of the recent research and comment.

The ultimate objective of education in a democratic society must be to facilitate the social, academic and identity development of young people in the increasingly complex society and world in which they live and function. While they should retain a sense of pride in their personal and cultural identity, children of all ethnic groups should also develop sensitivity and empathic awareness of the personal and cultural identities of others around them without feeling the need to retreat behind alienating barriers of cultural protectionism. This approach should meet the affective and cognitive needs of all groups as well as individuals in a plural society.

This book is in two distinct, yet related, sections. The first is concerned with a range of important and controversial issues. The second contains empirical evidence about the educational attainments of various groups of British Asian and Afro-Caribbean pupils.

The issues considered and the outcomes described are often presented in terms of membership of ethnic groups. Each of the authors is aware of this orientation. Acknowledging this should sensitize readers to Whitman's clarion call:

'I swear nothing is good to me that ignores individuals'.

PART 1
ISSUES

1 Issues in Multicultural Education

Gajendra K. Verma

In many Western countries there has been explicit concern in recent years about the emerging 'pluralist' composition of society. It has arisen out of the demographic, social and cultural changes brought about by the process of post-war migration. There have been, and continue to be, discussion and arguments as to the most appropriate way of responding to such changes. A major part of the debate has centred on the role of education.

In a multicultural, multiethnic society such as the UK the population is composed of a number of distinct social, cultural, religious and linguistic groups and this presents a new reality for the educational system as a whole. Attempts by some educationalists to analyze the nature of society and evolve an appropriate response have been constantly frustrated by the social context in which the system of education exists and operates. As we all know, an educational system does not exist in a historical and social vacuum. It functions within the framework of specific attitudes, values and norms as determined by the dominant culture.

The British educational system is no exception. Its deep *monocultural* orientation is evident in aims, objectives, contents, methods and the assessment procedures of formal education. For example, if we examine the syllabus of history, geography, religious education, art and other subjects we find that other countries and cultures, particularly non-Western, are often dismissed as 'primitive' and are of 'inferior' quality or irrelevant.

Our research with 9–13-year-old children showed that people from the Third World are perceived by white children as members of underdeveloped continents who are primitive, battling unsuccessfully against their environment (Verma and Mallick, 1984). In terms of economy, life-styles, eurocentrism and stereotyping, white children described people from the Third World in a negative way. The study also confirmed the general belief that the process of transmission of images and perceptions from book to child is mediated through the presence of the teacher who interprets the material to the child in varying ways, based on underlying assumptions.

Books are crucial resources in curriculum responses to the challenge of multiculturalism in British schools. Teachers are crucially important too in interpreting textbooks to pupils. Unfortunately, the evidence to date suggests that only a minority of teachers approach this task in an unbiased or unprejudiced way.

What we select, how we organize schooling, how teaching is implemented in a multicultural setting, all embody ethnocentric overtones to a lesser or greater degree. Our schooling also reflects the values and value orientations of our respective societies. It seems an inescapable fact that schooling has a lot to do with reinforcing and developing children's stereotyped attitudes towards other people from ethnic groups. Understanding the process may provide a clue to ways in which teachers can counter the serious effects of ethnocentrism.

The white children educated by the use of the monocultural curriculum will perceive their black peers through the lens of stereotypes. Many white teachers have also been educated in a similar environment and consequently share the children's insensitivity. It is not surprising therefore that many ethnic minority children under-achieve within the British educational system. Such a pattern emerged both in the Committee of Inquiry (1985) and in the Report of the Brent Independent Investigation (1986). There is sufficient evidence in the literature to suggest that the British educational system has so far failed to concern itself with the preparation of all individuals to live in a society composed of varied races, cultures, social norms and life styles — each different but interdependent.

Having sketched out the broad educational context we must now turn our attention to some of the issues in the education of ethnic minorities.

Issues in Schooling of Ethnic Minorities

Although we have used the term 'ethnic minorities' we shall be concentrating on Afro-Caribbeans and Asians, since the main issue central to the multicultural debate has been about the education of children of Afro-Caribbean and Asian origins in British schools. This has prompted a number of questions and debates about how these children are fitted to the prevailing education system and its expectations, and on the other hand, how the education system can best be modified to meet the particular needs of a multicultural society. Such debates have covered much more than educational issues, extending to, for instance, racial prejudice in society and the socio-economic political consciousness in the country that affects all individuals. However, our particular aim here is to examine some of the educational issues that affect educational attainments of ethnic minority pupils in British schools.

The general trend of most studies has been to suggest that children of Afro-Caribbean and Asian origins are performing less well than their white counterparts. Some researchers studying the area in depth have identified a wide range of factors involved in the process of educational attainment; they have also emphasized the complexity of the issue (Tomlinson, 1983; Verma, 1986). Parental and community concern over poor educational attainments of ethnic minority children, particularly West Indians, was one of the major contributing factors in the establishment of, first, the Rampton Committee in 1979 and its successor, the Swann Committee in 1981.

Among the questions that the Swann Committee considered was whether some ethnic groups underachieve within the British educational system. And if they do, what factors contribute to underachievement? The Committee examined a whole range of factors such as disadvantageous social and economic circumstances, parental attitudes, the school curriculum, the appropriateness of the assessment procedures used for special education placement, the needs of minority groups, racial prejudice inside schools and in society at large. The Swann Report explicitly reminds us that biases in the educational system have contributed to this failure of ethnic minority children to achieve their full potential (Committee of Inquiry, 1985). It further adds that the educational system can do justice by replacing the present monocultural with multicultural and antiracist education. Such an education, according to the Report, aims to cultivate equal respect for, and a sensitive understanding of, all cultures. (See Chapter 6.)

The Swann Report acknowledges that the ethnic minority children, particularly the West Indian and the Bangladeshis, grossly underachieve in British schools. Amongst many possible explanations it admits that racism in British society in general and in the schools in particular, is one of the most important reasons for this. The Report states that issues confronting ethnic minority children cannot be solved without changing the basic fabric of mainstream education.

It is clear from the analysis so far that in a plural society education should be appropriate to the needs and aspirations of all ethnic and cultural groups. In that sense multicultural education is the logical and practical extension of the philosophy of pluralism. However, there are both proponents and critics of the concept and practice of multicultural education. Perhaps the most optimistic view of multicultural education has been taken by the Rampton Committee (Committee of Inquiry, 1981,) which states that 'a theory and practice of a multicultural approach to education' exists (p. 71). On the other hand, Stone (1981) rejects multicultural education as a distraction from the primary function of schooling. She argues that it is poor schooling which has to be blamed for any educational problems experienced by black pupils in British schools. According to her, multicultural education is simply a sham, a cheap education by which the oppression of black children is compounded.

In spite of the negative evaluation of the idea of multicultural education by some writers an obvious advantage is that it avoids the unfortunate connotations associated with 'race'. Furthermore, the idea of multicultural education is likely to appeal to those who appreciate cultural diversity. However, a model of multicultural education based on the equal power of cultural and ethnic groups within a particular society, is intrinsically attractive, and refreshingly innovative in its implications for the reform of British society (Verma and Bagley, 1984).

Language and Multicultural Education

Few educationalists would disagree that language is the primary vehicle for the maintenance of one's own culture. Language is a means to achieve identity, and a means to recover self-esteem. Ghuman (1975), in comparing the qualities of thinking displayed by different cultural and ethnic groups in a multicultural context, concluded that:

> If we accept the important role of language in the development of higher cognitive processes, further attention has to be paid to the improvement of the children's oral and written language.

The most recent concept introduced in the field of multicultural education is 'Mother-tongue' teaching. On 25 July 1977 the Council of the EEC adopted the directive that ethnic minorities have a right to the maintenance of their home language and culture through the school system of a member-state.

The debate for and against mother-tongue teaching is still continuing. However, for some ethnic groups another language may have greater social prestige, for example, learning a community language. In spite of the negative reactions from certain sections of the British population, support for mother-tongue has come from several local education authorities.

For each child his or her native language is a precious birthright. In a multicultural society, therefore, a child's first language should be his or her traditional cultural language. English, the lingua franca, should be introduced when formal schooling begins; but the onset of schooling should not imply the subordination of the child's native language. That language too should be fostered within the educational system and incorporated into the curriculum of the multicultural school.

Attitudes of Teachers

Another issue closely bound up with multicultural education is the attitudes of teachers. There can hardly be a school in Britain today which does not contain some ethnic minority pupils. One of the functions of education is to prepare all pupils for life in a multicultural society, in which the identities and aspirations of all ethnic groups must be respected and balanced in a manner which is compatible with principles of social justice. If some teachers are racially prejudiced, either in an active or a passive manner, how can they fulfil their role as educators in a plural society?

Pupils are labelled as 'stupid' or 'bad' everyday — both on the basis of test scores, and on the basis of teachers' attitudes and perceptions. Research shows that this labelling process is even more evident where pupils come from ethnic minority groups. They are often stereotyped as being different and to some extent 'inferior', and this in turn influences teachers' attitudes and behaviour towards them. On the other hand, some teachers deliberately ignore the culture and ethnicity of their pupils and tend to impose values and norms of the dominant culture on all children.

Teacher attitudes and expectations are shown to be of primary significance with regard to achievement/underachievement of pupils. This is borne out by an analysis of data, drawn from the National Child Development Survey, on West Indian children (Bagley, 1982).

The findings showed that by the time some children were 7 years old, teachers' highly negative views had not only led to a marked degree of underachievement among them but such views had also led to a substantial number of black children being placed, or recommended for placement, in ESN schools.

Teacher expectation that ethnic minority pupils, particularly West Indians, are likely to achieve poorly at school has also been identified by the Rampton Inquiry (Committee of Inquiry, 1981).

> Again it has repeatedly been pointed out to us that low expectations of the academic ability of West Indian pupils by teachers can often prove a self-fulfilling prophecy. Many teachers feel that West Indians are unlikely to achieve in academic terms but may have high expectations of their potential in areas such as sport, dance, drama and art. If these particular skills are unduly emphasized there is a risk of establishing a view of West Indian children that may become a stereotype and teachers may be led to encourage these pupils to pursue these subjects at the expense of their academic studies.

It should also be mentioned that teachers do not label all black pupils as low achievers, but only particular kinds of black pupils. In a study by Bagley, Bart and Wong (1979), teachers were asked to rate the potential of their pupils. Some black pupils were rated as being of low potential while others were rated as being of high potential. The 'low potential' pupils, as rated by their teachers, tended to be from homes which were materially handicapped, where father might be absent, and where Creole, rather than standard English, was spoken.

However, teacher attitudes can seriously affect the academic performance of ethnic minority pupils in two main ways: by explicitly prejudiced interaction with them; and by the holding of low expectations of their abilities and achievement. Both are found among teachers who are members of the dominant culture in British schools (Giles, 1977).

Teachers need to develop a multicultural orientation so that they can act successfully and confidently in a plural society. The need to learn how to acknowledge, and if necessary, reconstruct their own attitudes and practices toward, and assumptions about, those from a culture different from their own.

Ethnic minority pupils in Britain have different identity structures than whites (Coleman *et al*, 1977). They have a more difficult struggle in educational, social and personal aspects of life than their parents; yet many of them are successful with regard to both achievement and identity development. Louden (1980) has argued that with the growth in numbers in minority communities, the setting of their 'locus of control' changes favourably. In schools where black or Asian groups are in the majority or even a substantial minority, they can more successfully guard against the demeaning slights of racism. A more recent research has failed to find any differences in levels of self-esteem between White, West Indian and Asian pupils in British schools (Verma, 1986).

Teachers sometimes seek to explain the behavioural and academic difficulties of ethnic minority pupils as a consequence of their having a poor self-concept and an identity problem. As a result a number of terms such as 'low self-esteem', 'identity crises' have been used by educators to explain poor educational attainment of ethnic minority pupils. In Britain some writers have suggested that West Indian pupils in particular lack confidence in their own abilities, have low expectations or depressed self-esteem. They also believe that West Indian pupils who perform less well at school are likely to have low self-esteem.

A study identified a group of West Indian pupils in British schools whose scores on standardized reading tests were as satisfactory as those of White, middle-class pupils (Bagley, Bart and Wong, 1979). Evidence showed that their family background and attitudes were markedly more independent, self-reliant and indeed hostile towards white society than those of other West Indian families. Those two groups of families also differed in terms of social class — the former were distinctly more middle-class than the latter. Therefore, it is at least possible that other attributes of middle-class family patterns were responsible for the better performance of their children.

Some writers suggest that the relationship between pupil and teacher in the multicultural classroom is a major factor contributing to the pupil's awareness of himself or herself (Verma and Bagley, 1982). This awareness, once assimilated into the pupil's self-concept may become an influential element in learning, and thus may operate as a significant factor in educational attainment. The findings of various studies show that poor self-esteem derived from school experiences tend to result in poor performance (See Verma, 1986).

Reflections

The issues outlined concerning the education of all ethnic groups in Britain will not go away overnight. There is a great diversity of cultural, ethnic and social patterns in British society. It is also true to say that the problems experienced by ethnic minorities in the British educational system are not new. Furthermore, there are other countries in the world where ethnic minorities face similar problems. The education of the English speakers in Quebec, of Walloons in Belgium and of Maoris in New Zealand are a few examples of situations where the education of ethnic minorities has been a political issue. Williams (1984) comments:

> The education of minorities is a contentious issue. In the struggle for educational resources it is both easy and understandable for the majority culture to press its own case, to foster a single system and to forget or pay lip-service to the different needs of the minority. When, as is happening more often, the minority community demands equal status in the education system for its own culture, its own customs and its own language, then the politicians anguish over power, and the purse-holders anguish over price. To the minority these are objections to be fought, for education is the theatre in which their future is decided. (p. 123)

Thus, in any analysis of issues in multicultural education it is difficult to separate the strands of political ideology and educational reality. Some critics interpret the recognition of and provision for cultural diversity within the education system as a threat to the dominant culture. It is not clear at the present time which direction the current drive towards multicultural education will take. However, there appears to be a positive commitment and response on the part of an increasing section of the British population to the idea of cultural pluralism. Unfortunately, Britain's official policies proceed gropingly, blindly and in similar directions to those which have led to failure and desperation in Ulster. Things may get worse before they get better!

References

BAGLEY, C. (1982) 'Achievement, behaviour disorder and social circum-stances in West Indian children and other ethnic groups' in VERMA, G.K. and BAGLEY, C. (Eds) *Self-concept, Achievement and Multicultural Education*, London, Macmillan.
BAGLEY, C., BART, M. and WONG, J. (1979) 'Antecedents of scholastic success in West Indian 10-year-olds in London' in VERMA, G.K. and BAGLEY, C. (Eds) *Race, Education and Indentity*, London, Macmillan.
BARROWN, J. (1987) *The Two Kingdoms: Standards and Concerns; Parents and*

Schools, Report of an Independent Investigation into Secondary Schools in Brent, 1981–1984, Brent, London Borough of Brent.

COLEMAN, J. (1977) 'Identity in adolescence: Present and future self-concepts', *Journal of Youth and Adolescence*, 6, pp 63–75.

COMMITTEE OF INQUIRY INTO THE EDUCATION OF CHILDREN FROM ETHNIC MINORITY GROUPS (1981) *West Indian Children in Our Schools*. (Rampton Report) Cmnd. 8273, London HMSO.

COMMITTEE OF INQUIRY INTO THE EDUCATION OF CHILDREN FROM ETHNIC MINORITY GROUPS (1985) *Education for All* (Swann Report) Cmnd. 9453, London: HMSO.

GHUMAN, P. (1975) *The Cultural Context of Thinking*, Windsor, NFER.

GILES, R. (1977) *The West Indian Experience in British Schools*, London, Heinemann.

LOUDEN, D.M. (1980) 'Self-esteem and locus of control: Some findings in immigrant adolescents in Britain', *New Community*, 6, pp 218–34.

STONE, M. (1981) *The Education of the Black Child in Britain*. Glasgow, Fontana.

TOMLINSON, S. (1983) *Ethnic Minorities in British Schools* London, Heinemann.

VERMA, G.K. with ASHWORTH, B. (1986) *Ethnicity and Educational Achievement in British Schools*, London, Macmillan.

VERMA, G.K. and BAGLEY, C. (Eds) (1982) *Self-concept, Achievement and Multicultural Education*, London, Macmillan.

VERMA, G.K. and BAGLEY, C. (Eds) (1984) *Race Relations and Cultural Differences*. London, Croom Helm.

VERMA, G.K. and MALLICK, K. (1984) 'Children's books and ethnic minorities' in VERMA, G.K. and BAGLEY, C. (Eds) *Race Relations and Cultural Differences*, London, Croom Helm.

WILLIAMS, P. (1984) *Special Education in Minority Communities*, Milton Keynes, Open University Press.

2 Monitoring the Reading Attainments of Children from Minority Ethnic Groups: LEA Practices

Peter Pumfrey

Introduction

The increased possibility of moving from one country and culture to another has led growing numbers of people to seek opportunities in other lands. According to the Office of Population Censuses and Surveys (OPCS), the population of Great Britain is estimated at 54,100,000. The total 'non-white' population in 1985 was 2,376,000. Many of these individuals and their families have been living in this country for extensive periods. Considerable numbers of immigrants have arrived in the relatively recent past. Others will continue to come.

There are many difficulties in reliably and validly categorizing citizens by ethnic group. Accepting these limitations, the OPCS figures indicate that there are nine such major groups in the UK ranging in size from 763,000 to 64,000. It is acknowledged that Britain has a long history of both immigration and emigration. As the rate of immigration into any culture by members of ethnic groups having different cultural values from the host community increases, tensions tend to be generated. Population movements present challenges to both the host country and the immigrant groups. Challenges can be seen as presenting problems and opportunities for both groups.

The diversity of minority ethnic groups in Britain and the educational progress of British children of parents of minority ethnic group origins is one important current public concern. To deal rationally and effectively with any challenge requires that, insofar as is possible, its nature and extent be determined. From this information base, constructive ways of responding to the focus of concern can be considered, implemented and evaluated. This chapter concerns one such issue.

Three related concerns bearing on the reading attainments of British children of parents of minority ethnic group origins initiated the enquiry. The first of these was the extent to which LEAs in England and Wales were undertaking authority-wide monitoring of reading standards. The second was whether LEAs were able to relate children's reading test scores to their parents' country of origin, in general, and in respect of British children of parents of West Indian origins, in particular. The third concern was the implications of the 1981 Education Act for LEAs concerning children who, in relation to reading, showed learning difficulties '... significantly greater than that of the majority of children of the same age' (DES, 1981, para. 4, p. 2.). This Act became operative as from 1 April 1983 and its implementation is far from complete.

Enabling children to read is recognized as one of our schools' curricular imperatives. Anyone unable to read in our society is seriously and progressively disadvantaged. Reading is an amplifier of human abilities. It is the power to comprehend the thought and feelings of others via the medium of print. Access to many fields of learning and, subsequently, to many occupations is barred to those unable to read proficiently. If it is suspected that national reading standards have deteriorated at any point in time, considerable concern is generated in society and in the teaching profession.

Over time, Britain has increasingly become a multicultural society (Commission for Racial Equality, 1978; Office of Population Censuses and Surveys, 1982, 1983a, 1983b, 1983c and 1986). One index of this is that a senior official from one large LEA has stated that 127 different languages are spoken by children attending the authority's schools. One of the largest of the ethnic minority groups represented in our schools is British children of parents of West Indian origins (in the interests of brevity this group hereafter will be referred to as the BWI group).

Considerable concern has been expressed about the educational attainments of BWI pupils in relation to the general population of pupils. The Rampton and Swann Reports have made the point forcibly (Committee of Inquiry into the Education of Children from Minority Ethnic Groups, 1981 and 1985). The relatively low reading attainments of BWI children had also been documented in a number of local surveys (Taylor, 1981). The longitudinal study begun in 1968 by the ILEA is one of the most substantial of these and involved testing pupils at the ages of 8, 10 and 15 years. A relative deterioration over time in the reading attainments of BWI pupils was reported. When possible social disadvantages such as parental occupation, family size, parent-school contact, free meals, length of education in Britain and the priority of school attended were allowed for statistically, it was concluded that the lower attainment of BWI pupils in the ILEA cannot be entirely explained by these factors alone (Mabey, 1981a and 1981b). This does *not* imply that other environmental factors might not contribute toward the remaining differences (DES, 1982; Murray and Dawson, 1984). Other large-scale local surveys have indicated that the situation is, in some respects, worse elsewhere in England (Phillips, 1979).

A study combining longitudinal and cross-sectional research methods was carried out in one town in the Midlands. The study examined the developmental status and school achievements of both minority and non-minority children from the pre-school years to late adolescence. BWI pupils' relatively low standards of reading existed from early in their educational careers. Such a situation culminates in a reduced access to higher education, employment and upwards mobility in our culture (Scarr *et al.*, 1983). The local authority involved has made positive responses to these findings (Roberts, 1984). A summary and update of this work is contained in the present book (see chapter 8). A recent comprehensive overview of the field continues to highlight the problems of low attainments for various ethnic minority group children (Mackintosh and Mascie-Taylor, 1986). An earlier longitudinal study of a nationally representative sample based on the National Child Development Study unfortunately contained only relatively low numbers of BWI pupils. Despite this, as found in other surveys, the importance of exposure to the English educational system is clearly shown in the relative superiority in reading of second generation BWI pupils over first generation WI pupils. Despite this hopeful sign, their reading attainments were still lower than those of the white indigenous group (Essen and Ghodsian, 1979; Ghodsian *et al*, 1980; Maughan and Dunn, 1986).

The parents of BWI pupils are understandably concerned at their children's relatively low reading attainments. It is an issue of more than sectional interest. It affects all groups. Various approaches aimed at increasing the reading attainments of BWI pupils are being actively advocated and pursued (Taylor, 1981; Stone, 1981; Pumfrey, 1983). Despite such efforts, plus the extensive amount of extra help given by primary school teachers to *all* pupils experiencing difficulties in learning to read, dissatisfaction by the black community with the educational system is increasing. For example, the Haringey Black

Pressure Group on Education is reported as accusing the primary school heads in the East of the borough of turning out barely literate and numerate pupils. 'The teaching of reading, writing, spelling and higher order language skills is your legal responsibility and you appear to be failing miserably with a substantial number of your children but especially black British children.' The same pressure group describes the secondary schools' examination results as 'appalling' and, in part, a consequence of the failure of the primary schools to teach their pupils to read (Venning, 1983). The reaction of the LEA as expressed by the Chief Education Officer is that the legitimate concerns raised by the pressure group were undermined by 'half-truths, inaccuracies and crude assumptions'. Their actions were seen as potentially counter-productive by the LEA.

Similar concern has been expressed in other LEAs where there are considerable numbers of BWI pupils. The London Borough of Brent is an example. The Brent Enquiry was set up as a response to such concern. The setting up of the enquiry in November 1983, was highly controversial and the full cooperation of the Authority's teachers was not obtained. A switch in political control of the local authority further complicated the work of the enquiry and led to divisions within the team. A minority report was submitted to the Director of Education in September 1985. Subsequently, a further change in political control took place. The findings and recommendations of the final report were published in 1986 and are summarized in a later chapter in this book (chapter 12). They themselves are controversial. The concern is real. It is justified. Action is required.

Should 'affirmative action', 'positive', 'benign' and 'reverse discrimination', be shown in the allocation of scarce resources in order to improve the relative reading attainments of BWI pupils? Evidence suggests that a very considerable input of resources is required to produce such changes (Woods, 1979). To do this, must the identification of groups by ethnic characteristics be carried out? Collecting statistics on race was stopped by the DES in the 1970s. The issue is a sensitive one. It has attendant dangers of which all concerned in this issue are well aware. Such a strategy has often been used to the detriment of groups so identified. The Rampton and Swann Committees acknowledge the problems created by the absence of statistics on the distribution of BWI pupils in our schools. Quoting from the former, 'Although some schools collect statistics on the ethnic origins of their pupils, there is little uniformity in the classifications used and it is difficult to make comparisons between one school and another, let alone gain anything approaching an overall picture' (DES, 1981, para. 3, p. 66). The situation had not changed by the time that the Swann Report was published. The reports advocate the value of ethnically based statistics to *all* parties concerned with education where such data are used to establish facts concerning the attainments and progress of ethnic minority groups in general. It was recommended in the Rampton Report that such data be collected as from 1 September 1982. The Commission for Racial Equality has also supported the collection of such data in order that decisions and policies be based on fact and not on inspired guesswork (Commission for Racial Equality, 1982). Concerning ethnic statistics, two DES working parties' reports, currently unpublished (March 1987), bear on this issue. One concerns teachers in service; the other relates to school pupils. The former has just been presented to the Secretary of State for Education and awaits his decision. The latter was presented to the Secretary of State some time ago. A statement was made in Parliament to the effect that it was his intention to put into operation a system for collecting ethnic statistics relating to pupils. To date, neither report has been formally published. As the working parties consisted of representatives of various interested groups, the content of the reports are quite widely known. Doubtless this inform-ation will be made public in a forthcoming Circular. The probability is that on both fronts a system of collecting ethnic statistics will be operated.★

Despite such backing from bodies keenly aware of the sensitive issues involved, a strong case can be argued against such a strategy. It is a case that has considerable support in some urban areas where a high proportion of BWI pupils live. Such reservations led to the deletion from the 1981 National Census of a question on race or ethnic origin. Estimates of the size of such groups in Britain have been derived from other sources. The inclusion in the *next* census of an ethnic question aimed at pinpointing areas of racial disadvantage and assisting with government resource allocation has subsequently been discussed by the All-party House of Commons Select Commi-ttee on Race Relations and Immigration. Both the Association of County Councils (ACC) and the Association of Metropolitan Author-ities (AMA) agree that the inclusion of such a question would be of value. Currently the Office of Population Censuses and Surveys is working with the CRE on this issue. Already at least one local autho-rity has adopted a policy of classifying all its employees according to

★The DES published a Draft Circular entitled *Ethnically-based Statistics on School Teachers* during the Autumn of 1987.

racial background and sex in order to implement a policy of equal opportunity in employment. The issue is controversial. At present, it appears likely that such a question will appear in the next census. Whether this will be of value to LEAs depends on the nature of the question and the availability of the data. It is likely to be of value only in general policy decisions.

A particularly sensitive aspect of the controversy pertinent to the present enquiry concerns the relative importance of environmental and genetic factors in accounting for the relationship between ethnic group and reading attainments. Not all groups of pupils having parents of minority ethnic group origins perform, on average, less well than the host population. One group of research workers has argued that a substantial proportion of the total population variance in intellectual performance, of which reading attainment is but one index, is genetically determined. In contrast, another group offers explanations based on differential adverse social pressures that impinge on ethnic minority groups to a far greater extent than on the population as a whole. In their extreme forms, neither the genetic nor the environmentalist position is particularly convincing to the disinterested observer (Scarr and Carter-Saltzman, 1982; Mabey, 1981a and 1981b). Even if a part of between-group variance in intellectual ability and/or reading attainment could be unequivocally shown to be genetic, the heritability of a trait does not mean that its expression is unaffected by environmental intervention. A valuable analysis of the causes and non-causes of BWI underachievement is summarized in the brief guide to the main issues in the Swann Report (Swann, 1985). The analysis identifies six major explanations. It then considers the assumptions underpinning such explanations, demonstrating the complexities of the situation and the ideological nature of the implicit political debate (*ibid*). On the other hand, by itself, the demonstration that a particular controllable environmental factor, such as teaching method increases reading attainments, is insufficiently precise. The pursuit of aptitude x instruction interactions (AIIs) remains a central educational concern. We need to know whether some methods/materials are, or are not, particularly beneficial to children from different cultural backgrounds. There are dangers here. The work on level I and level II abilities by Jensen and that on the availability of restricted and elaborated language codes by Bernstein, testifies to this. To date, this search for AIIs has not been marked by clear-cut results, but should not be abandoned on that score alone (Seitz, 1977; Stone, 1981). There are more recent studies showing possible AIIs (Naylor and Pumfrey, 1983; Freebody and Tirre, 1985). Such studies do not adequately address the issue of learning styles and cultural differences.

In England and Wales there are 104 LEAs. A Schools Council project 'Studies in the Multi–ethnic curriculum' included a survey of all LEAs in England and Wales. Seventy LEAs returned the question-naire. Seventeen replied by letter. Seven discussed the issues involved when visited by the researchers. Of these ninety-four LEAs, seven-teen said that they kept statistics so that they know how many of their pupils are from families of Asian, West Indian and other minority ethnic group origins (Little and Wiley, 1981, p. 26). The bases on which these records are kept varies. Some LEAs have continued using categories defined in the pre-1973 DES form 7 (i). Others have adapted them to suit their particular circumstances. According to the report, most LEAs in areas containing high and medium concentra-tions of families from ethnic minority groups considered that such data would be helpful in assessing special educational needs, in alloca-ting resources and in monitoring the relative progress of pupils. Some BWI parents are sceptical. The mean scores on standardized reading tests of groups of BWI pupils are typically significantly below the population norms. This may, in part, have contributed to what the parents of BWI pupils see as a disproportionate number of their children being placed in schools for the ESN(M). Presumably such placements are made in what was, at the time, seen to be the child's best interests. Such placements represent a much higher per capita financial investment in children's education than is the case in the ordinary state school system. Such placements demonstrate LEAs' concern. Is this misguided? There appears to be little evidence that the effects on BWI pupils' reading attainments is reflected in this increased investment. (It is accepted that such schools have wider goals than increasing reading attainments).

The 1981 Education Act (effective as from 1 April 1983) and its associated Circulars and Statutory Instruments are pertinent to the relatively low reading attainments of BWI pupils insofar as the iden-tification of needs and the provision of resources is concerned. Section 1 of the Act states that a child has special educational needs if he has significantly greater difficulty in learning than the majority of children of that age. Whilst this is clearly *not* the case in relation to reading attainments, for *all* BWI pupils, it is the case for a greater proportion of BWI pupils than those comprising the rest of the population of pupils. The operational and the legal definition of 'significantly greater difficulty ...' becomes crucial. It is known that, for example, the British Dyslexia Association sees the Act as opening an avenue towards additional resources to help those children who are the Association's particular concern. A similar stance *could* be adopted in relation to BWI pupils by their parents as part of a movement to obtain the resources that might reduce the gap between reading attainments and educational opportunities of BWI and other groups of pupils. The issue is a complex one to which there is unlikely to be any simple organizational or instructional solution. Authoritative legal interpretations of any of the provisions of the 1981 Act are *exclusively* a function of the Courts.

The Education (Special Educational Needs) Regulations 1983 became operative on 1 April 1983. Even prior to its coming into operation, a number of LEAs were involved in legal cases seeking to clarify their responsibilities in providing special resources for the assessment and alleviation of children's reading difficulties. LEAs are becoming increasingly involved in such litigation. Whilst litigation by itself cannot improve a child's reading attainments, it may facilitate the provision of resources that can help towards this end for children from *any* cultural background. The Act does not assume that a child has a learning difficulty 'because the language or form of language of his home is different from the language of instruction in his school' (DES, 1983, para. 70, p. 14). Thus, low reading attainments caused by such circumstances are not covered. If there is an adverse interaction between the BWI pupils' dialects and the materials with which they learn to read, the dialect-interference hypothesis, this would also appear to be excluded under the Act because of the words 'form of language'. Studies involving both host population (white) and BWI pupils in relation to this hypothesis indicate that it is a field requiring much more attention than it has received to date. One recent research involving the reading accuracy and comprehension of first-year secondary school pupils questions the validity of the dialect interference hypothesis at that age (Pumfrey and Lee, 1982).

The occupational consequences of BWI pupils' relatively low mean scores on standardized reading tests, are highlighted by the following example. It allows the matter to be roughly quantified. Assume that on a valid and reliable measure of reading ability with a mean of 100 and a standard deviation of 15 points, the variance in reading test scores at the end of compulsory education in the group of BWI pupils is distributed similarly to that in the general population at that age. On the basis of the various large local surveys that have been carried out, assume that the BWI pupils have a mean score of 87. This is rather less than one standard deviation below the population mean. In the general population, 50 per cent of pupils will have reading ages *equal to or above* their chronological ages. In the BWI group, the proportion reaching this level will be about 20 per cent. If one of the requirements of a job was that the holder be able to read at a level *at least* equivalent to the applicant's chronological age, the adverse occupational implications for BWI pupils are immediately apparent. In the general group of 16-year-old pupils, one in two of the pupils would have the reading attainments required for the job. In the BWI group, approximately one in five would meet the requirements. When linked to the examination requirements for entry to higher education, it is clear that relatively few BWI pupils would be in a position to continue studies leading to various professional qualifications. This appears to be a fact (Scarr *et al.*, 1983; Mabey, 1986). Such considerations have contributed to a demand in some areas for the provision of alternative schools for black pupils. They have also contributed to a 'back to basics' movement in terms of the curriculum.

Whilst the preceding example *is* an over-simplification based on assumptions that can be questioned, it does highlight an issue that concerns many individuals and groups in our society. If such a mean difference occurred at earlier ages, it indicates that a higher proportion of BWI children will have low reading attainments than is found in the general population of pupils. Where a school population was 50 per cent BWI and 50 per cent children with attainments equivalent to the general population norms, a higher proportion of BWI pupils is likely to be transferred to special schools established for the *benefit* of all children with learning difficulties. As was noted earlier, there is already considerable concern by the parents of BWI pupils and the organizations representing their interests that BWI pupils are over-represented in such schools. Current policies encourage the retention of children with reading difficulties in mainstream schools.

It has been argued that the mean differences on which the preceding argument is based reflect, in part, invalid instruments and testing procedures. This reservation cannot be ignored. It highlights dangers inherent in any testing programme and the interpretation of its results. Instances in which pupils from ethnic minority groups do achieve scholastically, albeit differentially, are important even though they too have methodological weaknesses (Driver, 1980a and 1980b; Franklin, 1984).

Method

Our concerns were, firstly, to establish the extent to which LEAs tested children's reading attainments at one or more age levels and, secondly, to determine whether LEAs could relate these attainments to pupils' ethnic origins in general and in respect of BWI pupils in particular. If such linking of data was possible, we were interested in the purposes to which it was put.

To obtain these data, a short five-item questionnaire was constructed. The first four questions could be answered by a 'Yes' or 'No' response. The fifth question allowed those LEAs able to compare the reading attainments of BWI and population standards within the LEA to specify the purposes to which the information was put. The questions used are shown in table 1 below.

Results

The answers to questions 1–4 for all LEAs are presented in table 2.

Table 1: Questions sent to all LEAs in England and Wales

Q.1. Does the LEA organize the testing of children's reading attainments across the authority at one or more age levels?   Yes   No

Q.2. Does the LEA record system enable children to be classified according to their parents' country of origin?   Yes   No

Q.3. When reading test scores are collected, can the LEA compare the reading attainments of children grouped according to their parents' country of origin?   Yes   No

Q.4. Is the LEA able to compare the reading attainments of children of parents of West Indian origin with the population reading standards in the LEA?   Yes   No

Q.5. If the answer to Q4 is 'Yes', for what purpose is this information used by the LEA? Please list the major purposes below.

Purposes (a) ....
....
(b) ....
....
(c) ....
....

Questionnaires were sent to all 104 LEAs in England and Wales. Replies were received from all LEAs, the final one being obtained in 1983. The authorities were informed that they would all receive a summary of the results of the research.

Peter Pumfrey

Table 2:   Responses to the four questions by all LEAs in England and Wales (100 per cent response: N = 104)

	Yes		No	
	Number	%	Number	%
Q1	81	77.9	23	22.1
Q2	7	6.7	97	93.3
Q3	4	3.8	100	96.2
Q4	7	6.7	97	93.3

Table 3:   Responses to the four questions by the ILEA and the London Boroughs (100 per cent response: N = 21)

	Yes		No	
	Number	%	Number	%
Q1	16	76.2	5	23.8
Q2	1	4.8	20	95.2
Q3	1	4.8	20	95.2
Q4	1	4.8	20	95.2

Table 4:   Responses to the four questions by Metropolitan District LEAs in England and Wales (100 per cent response: N = 36)

	Yes		No	
	Number	%	Number	%
Q1	30	83.3	6	16.7
Q2	3	8.3	33	91.7
Q3	1	2.8	35	97.2
Q4	3	8.3	33	91.7

Subsequent tables 3, 4 and 5 give separate analyses from the ILEA and London boroughs, the Metropolitan District LEAs and the Northern Metropolitan Counties. The possibility of different patterns in these organizational categories was of interest.

The seven LEAs answering 'yes' to questions 2 and 4 were *NOT* the same sub-set. Four LEAs answered 'yes' to both questions. Three LEAs who answered 'yes' to question 2 answered 'no' to the subsequent questions. Three LEAs who had answered 'no' to question 2 entered a *qualified* 'yes' for question 4. The qualifications all indicated that these data were not collected regularly for all pupils in authority-wide manner but had, on occasion, been collected for particular purposes.

Table 5: Responses to the four questions by non-Metropolitan counties
(100 per cent response: N = 47)

	Yes		No	
	Number	%	Number	%
Q1	35	74.5	12	25.5
Q2	3	6.4	44	93.6
Q3	2	4.3	45	95.7
Q4	3	6.4	44	93.6

Discussion

Political and popular demands that LEAs and schools demonstrate their accountability to the society that funds the service, have increased over the past decade. The use of various reading tests across schools within LEAs has been one means of obtaining evidence concerning standards and progress in one of the key aspects of the syllabus. The percentage of LEAs undertaking authority-wide testing of children's reading attainments at one or more age levels continues to increase. In 1973 the Bullock Committee contacted the then 146 LEAs in England and Wales prior to Local Authority re-organization. Ninety-three out of one hundred and forty-six (63.7 per cent) responded and fifty out of ninety-three (53.8 per cent) reported that they carried out objective testing of reading. At that time, authority-wide reading surveys were carried out by only a small number of LEAs. In 1970 eighteen out of ninety-three (19.4 per cent) did so, and by 1972 this had risen to thirty-seven out of ninety-three (39.8 per cent) (DES, 1975, p. 257).

In 1980 the SSRC funded the Evaluation of Testing in Schools Project. A questionnaire was sent to the 104 LEAs in England and Wales, and replies were obtained from ninety-six (92.3 per cent), eighty-eight (84.6 per cent) of whom completed the questionnaire. Of these, seventy-one out of the eighty-eight (80 per cent) reported '. . . regular authority-wide testing programmes for reading covering at least one age group (plus a further four who tested "English")' (Gipps and Wood, 1981).

In the present survey we were fortunate enough to obtain a response from all LEAs in England and Wales. The overall numbers and percentages of LEAs answering 'Yes' to Question 1 in tables 2 to 5 were eighty-one out of one hundred and four (77.9 per cent). Metropolitan District LEAs, thirty out of thirty-six (83.3 per cent), responded positively more frequently than ILEA plus the London Boroughs sixteen out of twenty-one (76.2 per cent) and the Non-Metropolitan Counties thirty-five out of forty-seven (74.5 per cent). Thus the figures are generally in agreement with the earlier work by Gipps and Wood in confirming a significant increase in LEA activity in this field since 1973. The use of reading tests in authority-wide testing is one increasingly accepted way of determining institutional accountability.

In passing, it should be remembered that during the years when most LEAs organized 11+ selective procedures, tests of verbal reasoning and/or of reading comprehension were frequently included in the battery of measures utilized. The results from such authority-wide testing were used in some LEAs to identify schools with high and low mean scores on the abilities tested and, where possible and appropriate, to provide advice and resources. However, typically, the content of the tests changed annually and, despite the annual standardizations, these changes in content prevented straightforward interpretations concerning changes in the pupils' reading standards in the LEA from year to year. The point is introduced to emphasize the LEAs' considerable and lengthy experience in organizing authority-wide testing of particular age groups on various tests.

Relatively few LEAs in the present survey reported having a record system that enabled children to be classified according to their parents' country of origin. The difficulties involved in such a process are very considerable. Only seven out of 104 (6.7 per cent) LEAs claimed to have such a system in the present survey. In the Schools Council project, Studies in a Multiethnic curriculum, seventeen out of ninety-four (20.2 per cent) LEAs said that they kept statistics enabling them to know the numbers of pupils of ethnic minority origins attending their schools. It would appear from our results that this number has *dropped* since 1981. That this should be so when the Rampton Report, the Commission for Racial Equality and the House of Commons Select Committee on Race Relations and Immigration had all advocated the potential value of such information, is an interesting reflection on the reaction of LEAs to the issue. They are keenly aware of the point made earlier by Taylor that '. . . if data on children of ethnic minority group origin were to be ascertained once again it would be necessary to reassure the West Indian community, especially parents, of the importance of such an exercise as a means of helping to establish the correct provision for the children's needs' (Taylor, 1981, p. 12). Many BWI pupils' parents believe that their children's relatively low reading attainments require action. The causes of this situation are far from clear. What can be done, and by whom, to improve the situation is equally complex. It is a situation in which oversimplified analyses and interventions are likely to be advocated. A sound system would have to recognize that the distinction between 'immigrant' referring to West Indians and 'indigenous' meaning white British is outdated. The British-born children of parents of West Indian origins, the second generation, *are* indigenous. A more promising classification, if one is eventually adopted, might more appropriately distinguish between first and second generation immigrants from various ethnic minority groups. Even this approach may have racialist overtones (Taylor, 1981).

The answers to question 3 show that only four out of 104 LEAs (3.8 per cent) are able to compare the reading attainments of children grouped according to their parent's country or origin. It is therefore surprising to find that seven out of 104 LEAs (6.7 per cent) report that they are able to compare the reading attainments of children of parents of West Indian origin with the population reading standards in the LEA. One might expect that the number answering 'yes' to question 3 would represent a ceiling to the number of LEAs responding 'yes' to question 4. One explanation is that what had been done on one occasion was not regular practice.

Examination of the small number of LEAs answering question 4 in the affirmative shows that four out of seven answered 'yes' to questions 2 and 3 also. The three LEAs who had answered 'no' to questions 2 and 3 but 'yes' to question 4 referred to:

(i) 'A recently commissioned research project in *one* area in cooperation with the local Community Relations Council'. The purpose to which these data will be put is 'to help us introduce programmes designed to help West Indian and Asian pupils improve their educational achievement'.

(ii) 'Two longitudinal studies have been carried out'. The information obtained was used for 'identifying areas of difficulty and to acquire knowledge relating to our LEA'. It also provided 'a base-line against which to measure future changes'.

(iii) Although a third LEA answered 'yes' to question 4, no answer was given to question 5.

Thus, for only two of these three LEAs can we understand the nature of the involvement that explains their responses to the questionnaire.

Turning to the four LEAs answering 'yes' to questions 2, 3 and 4, we can note the purposes to which the information enabling the reading attainments of BWI and the population standards to be compared in these authorities was used. These purposes were:

    (i)   'General information only'.

    (ii) 'For the deployment of remedial service support staff to schools.'

          'For the deployment of ethnic minority support services.'

          'For the planning and monitoring of services to ethnic minorities/children with learning difficulties in the LEA.'

    (iii) 'Following screening at 7+ years, reading scores of *all* children are reviewed by Advisory, School Psychological and Special Educational Needs Support Services with a view to:

          interpreting results and implications regarding special needs; diagnosis;

          prescription;

          liaison with other agencies, including parents;

          resource-materials/staffing;

          in-service training needs;

          evaluation and follow-up as child progresses through school.'

          'School staffs assume similar responsibilities to review, provide and monitor progress as children transfer from school to school.'

    (iv) 'It's not really used. For your interest, the attainments of BWIs in (LEA) *don't* differ to any extent from the rest of the population.'

Though only few in number, these comments support the belief that the purposes of underpinning the collection of such data are typically intended to help the LEA to become more informed about its population and to carry out its work more effectively. They are not guilty of unfair discrimination.

The final comment presented above is an important one. Further details are currently being sought.

Research carried out in a north-west industrialized conurbation and involving over 5000 secondary school pupils attending ten comprehensive schools has shown that the BWI pupils' reading attainment scores, when unadjusted, do show a mean score significantly lower than the other groups. However, when allowance is made statistically for a range of associated variables, the difference becomes '. . . barely or non-significant' (see chapter 11). The methodology and its interpretation are both complex and controversial.

Turning to comments made by other LEAs, a number emphasized that they had no sizeable ethnic minority groups. Others specified considerable groups of children of parents of Indian, Pakistani
and a wide variety of other minority ethnic origins. Additional comments reveal important matters of principle relating to race relations
in this country and to the implications of computer storage of survey
data by LEAs.

> We have virtually no children of West Indian origin, but I
> would be very concerned about any *apartheid* recording if we
> had.

> Our data at 6+, 8+ and 10+ are computer stored . . . but no
> sensitive information on children's background is collected . . .

The identification of pupils by the ethnic origin of their parents poses
a number of different but related political, ethnical, economic and
educational dilemmas to different interest groups in our society. LEAs
will have to decide whether such identification of pupil groups,
and the linking with reading attainments is, on balance, justified.
Whatever course is followed, the importance of *Education for All*
and the case for differential interventions to meet identified needs of
any section of pupils, must be balanced. With limited resources and
unlimited demands on LEAs, the challenge is a major one.

Conclusion

From the results it appears that no more than four out of 104 LEAs
organize authority-wide testing of reading at one or more age levels
and are also able to compare the reading attainments of BWI pupils
with the population reading standards in the LEA.

Those LEAs able to collect and analyze data in this way do so for
reasons that appear to be in the interests of pupils who experience
reading difficulties. At least one very large LEA collects information
on pupils' ethnic origins and uses this to devise an index of deprivation on which resource allocation is based.

Irrespective or cultural or ethnic background, not all pupils will
learn to read with equal facility and competence. Inter- and intra-
individual and group differences in language and reading attainments
continuously challenge the organization and methodologies of
education. If decision-making by LEAs in relation to the identification
of children's educational needs and the allocation of resources is to be

made more explicit, individuals and groups of pupils experiencing difficulties in learning to read must be identified. The effects of intervention must also be monitored if an LEA is to be seen to be professionally accountable to the population it exists to serve. The 1981 Education Act has considerable legal implications for LEAs in this field. The Education Reform Bill (1987) will produce more.

Summarizing, the case for collecting data on reading attainments and on ethnic origins is a strong one. It must be stressed that in such work we are often concerned with mean differences between groups of children. This must not blind us to the very considerable range of inter-individual differences within groups. The importance of the individual cannot be ignored. He or she must not disappear in the statistically laundered blandness of group mean scores.

In England and Wales there is no uniform system used by all LEAs to identify children's ethnic origins. Only a minority of LEAs collect such data in their own ways. (It would not be easy to devise and operate a nationally acceptable scheme). Most LEAs do undertake authority-wide monitoring of reading attainments for entire year groups. From these three facts it is clear that hardly any LEAs are able to compare the reading attainments of BWI pupils compared with the population standards. As noted earlier, we have found only four in the present survey. The Assessment of Performance Unit (APU) has abandoned its attempt to collect such data. The problems of devising an acceptable means of making reliable and valid assessments of the reading attainments, progress and educational needs of BWI pupils are formidable, but far from insurmountable.

One solution is to sidestep the issue because of its political sensitivity coupled with a belief that the cost benefits ratio to all involved would be too high both financially and in terms of its effects on race relations. To follow this line could be to deny the possibility that the teaching styles and methods typically used in urban schools may be '... particularly unhelpful to West Indian children' (Stone, 1981). This is but one of a number of lines currently being explored by research workers. A number of promising practices have been identified (Pumfrey, 1983; Committee of Inquiry into the Education of Children from Minority Ethnic Groups, 1985).

BWI pupils and their parents are understandably resentful of the relatively poor reading attainments the children currently tend to achieve. So too are the parents of other groups of children whose reading attainments are low, irrespective of ethnic background.

Discrimination is a word that has acquired many negative con-notations. Our concern must be with discriminating fairly (Runnymede Trust and the British Psychological Society, 1980). The difficulty is that views of what constitutes 'fairness' in education differ greatly. Further, the concept of 'underachievement' in reading is not simple. There are many different ways in which the concept can be operationally defined, but no agreement as to which is the most valid.

In the interests of the children and society that LEAs exist to serve, on balance it is doubtful whether a continued self-imposed ignorance of the relationship between reading attainment and ethnic group is desirable. Perhaps our current state of knowledge represents a form of phenomenological bliss not to be disturbed by empiricism? If the facts were more clearly established, would not this help rational decision-making concerning the identification of needs, resource development and allocation?

References

COMMISSION FOR RACIAL EQUALITY (1978) *Ethnic Minorities in Britain: Statistical Background*, London, Commission for Racial Equality.

COMMISSION FOR RACIAL EQUALITY (1982) *Evidence presented to the Home Affairs Select Committee of Members of Parliament.* 29 November.

COMMITTEE OF INQUIRY INTO THE EDUCATION OF CHILDREN FROM MINORITY ETHNIC GROUPS (1981) *West Indian Children in our Schools* (Rampton Report) Cmnd. 8273, London, HMSO.

COMMITTEE OF INQUIRY INTO THE EDUCATION OF CHILDREN FROM MINORITY ETHNIC GROUPS (1985) *Education for All* (Swann Report), Cmnd. 9453, London, HMSO.

DAWSON, A.L. (1984) 'Characteristics, attainments and attitudes of secondary school pupils of European, Asian and Afro-Caribbean descent', unpublished PhD thesis, University of Manchester.

DEPARTMENT OF EDUCATION AND SCIENCE (1975) *A Language for Life.* (Bullock Report), London, HMSO.

DEPARTMENT OF EDUCATION AND SCIENCE (1981) *Education Act, 1981*, Circular 8/81, London, HMSO.

DEPARTMENT OF EDUCATION AND SCIENCE (1982) *A Classification of Local Education Authorities by Additional Educational Need (Cluster Analysis)*, Statistical Bulletin 8/82, London, Department of Education and Science.

DEPARTMENT OF EDUCATION AND SCIENCE (1983) *Assessments and Statements of Special Educational Needs*, Circular 1/83. London, Department of Education and Science.

DEPARTMENT OF EDUCATION AND SCIENCE (1987) *Ethnically-based Statistics on School Teachers*, London, HMSO.

DRIVER, G. (1980a) 'How West Indians do better at school (especially girls)', *New Society*, 17 January, pp 111–4.

DRIVER, G. (1980b) *Beyond Underachievement: Case Studies of English, West Indian and Asian School Leavers at 16 plus*, London, Commission for Racial Equality.

ESSEN, J. and GHODSIAN, M. (1979) 'The children of immigrants: School performance', *New Community*, 1, 3, pp 422–9.

FRANKLIN, A. (1984) 'Contemporary psychology in a multicultural society', *Educational and Child Psychology*, 1, 1, pp 5–13.

FREEBODY, P. and TIRRE, W.C. (1985) 'Achievement outcomes of two reading programmes: an instance of aptitude-treatment interaction, *British Journal of Educational Psychology*, 55, 1, pp 53–60.

GHODSIAN, M., ESSEN, J. and RICHARDSON, K. (1980) 'Children of immigrants: Social and home circumstances', *New Community*. VIII, 3, pp 195–205.

GIPPS, C. and WOOD, R. (1981) 'The testing of reading in LEAs: The Bullock Report seven years on', *Educational Studies*, 7, 2, pp 133–43.

LITTLE, A. and WILLEY, R. (1981) *Multi-ethnic Education: The Way Forward,* Schools Council Pamphlet 18, London, Schools Council.

MABEY, C. (1981a) *Black British Literacy: A Study of Reading Attainment of London Black Children from 8 to 15 years*, RS776/81, London, ILEA.

MABEY, C. (1981b) 'Black British literacy: A study of reading attainment of London black children from 8 to 15 years', *Educational Research*, 23, 2, pp 83–95.

MABEY, C. (1986) 'Black pupils' achievements in inner London', *Educational Research*, 28, 3, pp 163–73.

MACKINTOSH, N.J. and MASCIE-TAYLOR, C.G.N. (1986) 'West Indian and Asian Children's educational attainments', paper read at the symposium on Educational Attainments and Minority Ethnic Groups held at the annual conference of the British Psychological Society, University of Sheffield.

MAUGHAN, B., DUNN, G. and RUTTER, M. (1986) 'Black pupils' progress in secondary school', paper read at the symposium on Educational Attainments and Minority Ethnic Groups held at the annual conference of the British Psychological Society, University of Sheffield.

MURRAY, C. and DAWSON, A. (1984) *Five Thousand Adolescents*, Manchester, University of Manchester Press.

NAYLOR, J.G. and PUMFREY, P.D. (1983) 'The alleviation of psycholinguistic deficits and some effects on the reading attainments of poor readers: a sequel', *Journal of Research in Reading*, 6, 2, pp 129–53.

OFFICE OF POPULATION CENSUSES AND SURVEYS (1982) *Sources of Statistics on Ethnic Minorities*, OPCS Monitor PP1 82/1, London, Office of Population Censuses and Surveys.

OFFICE OF POPULATION CENSUSES AND SURVEYS (1983a) *Labour Force Survey: Country of Birth and Ethnic Origin*, OPCS Monitor LF8 83/1, London, Office of Population Censuses and Surveys.

OFFICE OF POPULATION CENSUSES AND SURVEYS (1983b) *Births by Birthplace of Parent 1981*, OPCS Monitor FM1 83/2, London, Office of Population Censuses and Surveys.

OFFICE OF POPULATION CENSUSES AND SURVEYS (1983c) *Births by Birthplace of Mother 1981: Local Authority Areas*, Monitor FM1 83/3, London, Office of Population Censuses and Surveys.

OFFICE OF POPULATION CENSUSES AND SURVEYS (1986) *Labour force Survey 1985: Ethnic Group and Country of Birth*, OPCS Monitor LFS 86/2 and PP1 86/3, London, Office of Population Censuses and Surveys.

PHILLIPS, C.J. (1979) 'Educational under-achievement in different ethnic groups', *Educational Research*, 21, 2, pp 116–30.

PUMFREY, P.D. (1983) 'The reading attainments of British children of parents of West Indian origins: Challenge and response', *Reading*, 17, 2, pp 111–24.

PUMFREY, P.D. and LEE, J. (1982) 'Cultural group, reading attainments and dialect interference', *Journal of Research in Reading*, 5, 2, pp 133–46.

ROBERTS, J.R. (1984) 'The relative development and educational under-achievement of ethnic minority children in a Midlands town', *Educational and Child Psychology*, 1, 1, pp 14–22.

RUNNYMEDE TRUST AND THE BRITISH PSYCHOLOGICAL SOCIETY (1980) *Discriminating Fairly: A guide to Fair Selection*, Report by the Runnymede Trust/ British Psychological Society Joint Working Party on Employment Assessment and Racial Discrimination, London, Runnymede Trust and the British Rsychological Society.

SCARR, S., CAPARULO, B., FERDMAN, B., TOWER, B. and CAPLAN, J. (1983) 'Developmental status and school achievements of minority and non-minority children from birth to 18 years in a British Midlands town', *British Journal of Developmental Psychology*, 1, 1, pp 31–8.

SCARR, S. and CARTER-SALTZMAN, L. (1982) 'Genetics and intelligence' in STERNBERG, R.J. (Ed) *Handbook of Human Intelligence*, Cambridge, Cambridge University Press.

SEITZ, V. (1977) *Social Class and Ethnic Group Differences in Learning to Read*, Newark, NJ, International Reading Association.

STONE, M. (1981) *The Education of the Black Child in Britain*, Glasgow, Fontana.

SWANN, M. (1985) *Education for All: A Brief Guide to the Main Issues of the Report*, London, HMSO.

TAYLOR, M. (1981) *Caught Between: A Review of Research into the Education of Pupils of West Indian Origin*, Windsor, NFER-Nelson.

VENNING, P. (1983) '"Menacing" warning sent to Haringey heads over exams', *Times Educational Supplement*, 11 February, p. 5.

WOODS, J. (1979) *The Relationship Between Reading Progress and Extra Help in Reading*, RS. No. 719/78, London, ILEA.

3 Developing Bilingual Children's English in School

Tony Kerr and Martin Desforges

Introduction

Many British children now have knowledge of two or more languages before they enter school. This potential foundation for achievement may easily be turned into a handicap by an inappropriate response. Some children may quite wrongly be referred for psychological advice because of slow progress in basic academic skills. If psychologists and teachers understand the principles involved in bilingual development, they will be able to create conditions to ensure a good rate of academic progress. If they do not, they may assume specific learning difficulties where none exist.

In addressing this chapter to monolingual psychologists and teachers, we are aware of some limitations and omissions. We have tried to review the major changes in British educational approaches to bilingual children over the last twenty years, to look at some of the relevant research findings, and to discuss the main factors that must be considered when suggesting help for children of any age who are learning English as a second language. We have not considered in detail the question of how bilingual children's English development can be helped by using their home languages in school, nor the undoubted value of children developing their other languages. These are vital matters, but we feel that they warrant a more extended discussion than can be included here.

Changing Educational Responses to Minority Ethnic Groups

Thirty years ago, ethnic minority groups from New Commonwealth countries were seen as having little influence on the indigenous population. Their presence was often regarded as temporary, or it was assumed that if they wished to remain in Britain they would be assimilated into British society, with the eradication of their separate languages and cultures. Although proficiency in English as a second language (ESL) was seen as the key to the assimilation of immigrant groups into British society, there was little or no ESL teaching, and pupils were left to pick up English as best they could. There was no evidence that this was successful (Tomlinson, 1980), and subsequently there was widespread concern at the slow rate of educational progress made by many children from minority ethnic groups (Goldman, 1973; Little, 1975).

Later on, however, it was recognized that ethnic minority groups were experiencing difficulties within the education system. The predominant response to these difficulties was, in effect, a policy of segregation (Houlton and Willey, 1983). ESL needs were met by setting up special language centres, and children remained in these centres until it was felt that they had sufficient skill in using English to cope in mainstream school. Often the centres worked hard to ensure their pupils quickly developed self-confidence, a sense of security and high motivation in their new environment, but were judged by others in the system largely on their ability to give children complete proficiency in English in a very short time.

Effects on the System

The setting-up of the specialized language centre had an unfortunate effect. Many teachers were relieved that responsibility had passed to a specialist service. At the same time, the skills and competence of ordinary teachers were devalued by the implication that they had no role in ESL teaching (*ibid*). It was thought that the specialist language centres would ensure that children had all the necessary skills to cope in ordinary classrooms, and that once they returned, their language 'deficit' would have been made good.

Problems often occurred when children returned to mainstream and it was found that although language centre staff had judged the pupil able to cope, the mainstream staff did not. Obviously, different criteria were being used, and the functional uses of language needed to survive in the school organization, and cope with the varied academic curriculum of mainstream schools, were not always the same as those used to assess progress in language centres. These differences of opinion often led to the conclusion that a particular child did not have

Figure 1: Multicultural education — stages of development

This diagram summarizes major trends. Different authorities, and schools within individual authorities, are progressing through these stages at different rates.

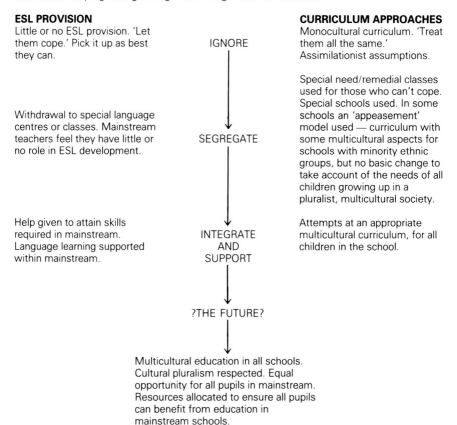

ESL PROVISION

Little or no ESL provision. 'Let them cope.' Pick it up as best they can.

IGNORE

CURRICULUM APPROACHES

Monocultural curriculum. 'Treat them all the same.' Assimilationist assumptions.

Withdrawal to special language centres or classes. Mainstream teachers feel they have little or no role in ESL development.

SEGREGATE

Special need/remedial classes used for those who can't cope. Special schools used. In some schools an 'appeasement' model used — curriculum with some multicultural aspects for schools with minority ethnic groups, but no basic change to take account of the needs of all children growing up in a pluralist, multicultural society.

Help given to attain skills required in mainstream. Language learning supported within mainstream.

INTEGRATE AND SUPPORT

Attempts at an appropriate multicultural curriculum, for all children in the school.

?THE FUTURE?

Multicultural education in all schools. Cultural pluralism respected. Equal opportunity for all pupils in mainstream. Resources allocated to ensure all pupils can benefit from education in mainstream schools.

a language problem, but more basic learning difficulties, and special education was sometimes seen as the solution. Educational psychologists involved in this process often used assessment techniques with a basic cultural bias, making it likely that ethnic minority children would perform badly, thereby supporting the notion that learning difficulties were the reason for failure to make progress in basic school attainments.

Recent Research

In recent years research on second language acquisition has produced a number of interesting findings which allow a fuller understanding of these problems. Traditionally second language learning was seen, even in some language centres, as primarily the acquisition of linguistic structures and knowledge of grammar — the variety of tenses of verbs, irregular forms of verbs, ability to conjugate verbs, transformation of sentences from affirmative to negative, active to passive, statements to interrogatives. Yet pupils and teachers were painfully aware that ability to handle grammatical structures may indicate nothing about the ability to use language in everyday life.

The learning of a language must take full account of its use, and teaching should start from the needs of the learner. Clearly, basic oral and literacy skills can be gained without a formal knowledge of linguistic structures — this is how we all learn our first language. However, there is often an assumption that when individuals have acquired this basic competence they have 'learned English'. This reflects a failure to recognize the important differences between language proficiency in face-to-face oral communication and those involved in academic, literacy-based skills (see Cummins, 1980 and 1981).

Figure 2 illustrates this view of language tasks. Context-embedded language proficiency refers to the ability to understand and be understood in situations where the verbal message is supported by a wide range of situational and paralinguistic cues (gestures, facial expression, intonation, etc.). Context-reduced proficiency is concerned with the ability to handle language when the range of non-linguistic supports is much reduced (for example, reading a book with no pictures, writing an essay). Context-embedded communication is more typical of the world outside school, whereas many classroom tasks tend towards the context-reduced end of the continuum. Learning in context-reduced, classroom situations requires more metalinguistic knowledge than coping with interpersonal communications (see Donaldson, 1978; Wells, 1981).

A further dimension is added when we consider the cognitive complexity of the tasks (the amount of information that must be processed, related to the prior knowledge and experiences of the individual). As skills are mastered they become less cognitively demanding, and some skills will be mastered faster than others. Many pupils will acquire context-embedded skills in English very quickly, but this does not necessarily mean that they have sufficient proficiency in the context-reduced, cognitively demanding aspects of English required to survive and progress in mainstream school without second stage language support. Studies from North America (Cummins, 1980, 1981 and 1982) suggest that although it may only take up to two

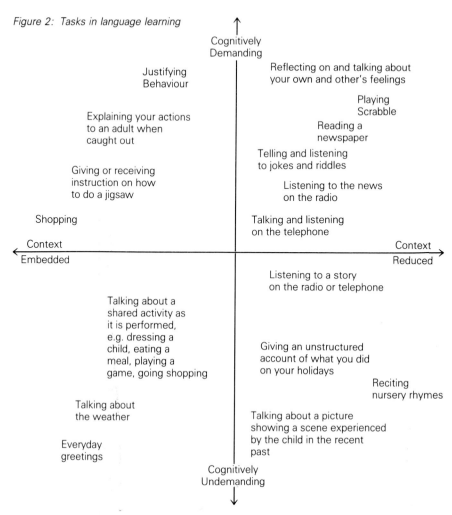

Figure 2: Tasks in language learning

years to acquire the skills needed to be fluent in face-to-face oral communication, it may take between five and seven years to acquire the full range of skills needed to cope in a context-reduced situation (see figure 3). This is supported by the work of Mabey (1981), who found that it was not until the secondary stage of education that many Asian pupils achieved reading scores comparable with native English speakers.

If a child appears to be fluent on the daily social routines of the classroom (which are often cognitively undemanding and embedded in context), it is easy to assume a similar level of language skills across the board (this is known as the facade effect). When the child performs badly on more difficult and abstract tasks, where there is less support from context, it is easy to assume that the failure is due to

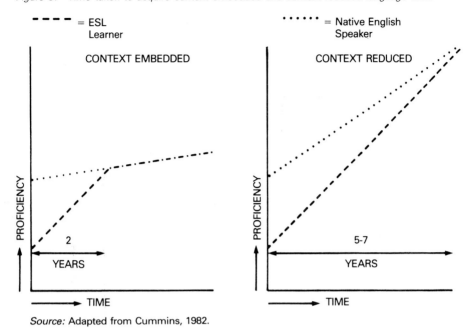

Figure 3: Time taken to acquire context embedded and context reduced language skills

Source: Adapted from Cummins, 1982.

learning difficulties rather than lack of appropriate language skills, and special education may appear necessary.

ESL Support in Mainstream Schools

The long time needed to gain adequate levels of context-reduced competence has important implications for the provision of support. If it takes five to seven years to achieve the underlying skills and competence comparable with native English speakers, then the short-term placements in language centres can only begin the process, and it follows that all teachers will need to help in developing the English of second-stage learners. Further, if we accept a functional approach to language skills, it make more sense to offer long-term support within mainstream, where a pupil will have more opportunities, and be better motivated to acquire the language necessary for academic progress and social integration. Prolonged separation of second language learners from the broad curriculum followed by all other pupils cannot be justified, since it leads to both curriculum and social learning being impoverished, with obvious effects on intellectual and social development (Barnes, 1976). Exposure to appropriate models is an important aspect of language learning, and there are obvious benefits from being exposed to the richer diversity of English in the mainstream school, provided that the required level of support is available. ESL support has then to be seen as part of a policy for language development which involves all teachers within a school, with specialist help and support from teachers with knowledge and skills in this field. This implies a more complex notion of appropriate language support throughout the curriculum and throughout the pupil's school day. The level and type of support required will depend on the linguistic competence of the pupil and the nature of the task being undertaken (see Little and Willey, 1981). There are some encouraging developments in changing the style and organization of ordinary classrooms, such as team teaching, cooperative teaching, collaborative learning. These are by no means universal, however.

Pupils need language as a tool for learning although the level of oracy and literacy skills required will be different in different curriculum areas. A careful analysis must be made to determine the nature and level of support required in each area (see Chamot, 1983). This process should involve all staff, to ensure that the nature of the language needs is understood, and appropriate action taken. In this way, the role of the ESL teacher then changes to one of support and service agent within mainstream school, helping colleagues to modify the reading and language tasks of their subject curricula.

First and Second Language Development

Most teachers would recognize the learning and development of a child's first language as being of central importance throughout the curriculum at both primary and secondary level, and a task in which all teachers are necessarily involved. This knowledge and experience can also be applied to second language learning as there are many similarities between first and second language development. For both first and second language users, meaning is the key to linguistic development. Children learn language largely through an active process of putting together the bits of language they know, rather than by exact imitation of sentence models. The main purpose of language is the communication of meaning, and people use whatever means are available to understand and communicate the meaning of a message. Children do not begin by uttering perfectly formed, grammatically correct sentences when learning a language. They produce a great deal of incomplete or non-standard language which they gradually correct by themselves through an approximation of the adult/native speaker model, with many omissions, overgeneralizations of grammar, pronunciation and vocabulary.

With second language learners, where the process of language-acquisition has already taken place in the mother tongue, there is the additional tendency to transfer patterns and meanings from the first language into the second. These can often be inappropriate; for example, since there is only one word for 'he' and 'she' in many North Indian languages, speakers of those languages who are learning English often use one or the other word in all situations: Jamaican Creole speakers might write or say 'Yesterday I walk to school' because in the first language the standard English past tense marker (in this case, -ed) is not used; English speakers experience difficulty pronouncing the French r sound.

In both first and second language learning there is often a delay in the onset of speech, sometimes called the silent period. Children need to listen to a great deal of language and make some sense of it before they are ready to talk. The implications for ESL teaching are clear. More time and attention should be given to listening activities at the beginning stages, and children should not be forced to speak until they feel ready to do so; they should, of course, be encouraged. It is important that opportunities for speaking are created by appropriate structuring of activities within the classroom.

Young children beginning to talk do so for a purpose (to request something, to get information, to express emotions). When these linguistic functions are not fundamental to second language learning, children lose interest and are difficult to motivate. They need an immediate and practical purpose to which they can put the new language. Teachers can create situations in which the new language is seen as immediately useful (making friends, playing, making excuses, explaining intentions, requesting information, learning how to get out of trouble. etc.). Increasing motivation to develop an insight into the use and purpose of the new language is of crucial importance.

What Can Be Done in Schools

In the light of the foregoing, let us consider what can be done in schools to help children learning English as a second language. There are five groups of factors that we shall consider, arranged in approximate order from those least open to school influence to those most open. They are:

— intelligence
— previous knowledge and experience
— motivation
— self-confidence and anxiety
— linguistic and related factors.

There is one fundamental matter that affects all five factors — the question of bilingualism. For most children from bilingual backgrounds it is a compromise to use anything less than a bilingual approach in which both languages are vehicles of learning. Nevertheless, monolingual teachers working in accordance with the principles outlined below can go a long way towards meeting the language needs of bilingual children. Although some of what follows may apply to only one particular age range, we feel that the underlying principles are very similar, so we have not divided out comments up according to age.

Intelligence

The classroom teacher has an important part to play in:

(i) creating the right conditions for children to display the full range of their intelligence by providing a classroom where the atmosphere and tasks develop all the skills a child already possesses;

(ii) ensuring that children's intelligence is not judged on superficial features. It is very easy to:
— underestimate the intelligence of poor speakers of English;
— overestimate the intelligence of fluent speakers. Their apparent understanding and social skills may mask gaps in their ability to cope when there is less support from context, for example, in academic tasks.

Research has shown that parents and teachers typically do both of the above. Similarly psychologists have been shown to make authoritative but logically indefensible recommendations (Cummins, 1982).

Previous Knowledge and Experience

It is often difficult to obtain detailed information about these, yet they are very important determiners of a child's current performance. We feel it is just as important for older as for younger pupils to follow the good educational principle of starting from where the child is, and building from his or her current skills. It is equally true that teachers cannot, except by chance, enable the child to derive maximum benefit from their efforts unless they know the approaches, aims and materials used by others who have taught the child, so it is important to find this out.

Motivation

This is the level where the teachers start to have real possibilities of influence. There is rarely any lack of 'external' motivation to learn English. Thanks to its status, both in the UK and overseas, parents and children usually agree with teachers on the central importance of learning this language. The newcomer to school may not at first be certain that he or she really wants to learn English, but this internal motivation can rapidly grow from the child's desire to make sense of his or her surroundings, to be part of a social group, and to please adults, so long as the teacher has provided a climate where the child feels accepted.

Specific motivation within a classroom may be more of a problem. Even if you know a child is keen to be able to speak English, you will still need to ask of your particular classroom or teaching arrangements:

— is the child motivated to learn in these surroundings? with these materials? with these other children? with these teachers?
— does the child see the point of what we are doing?
— can the child see that progress is being made?
— am I helping the child meet what he or she sees as his or her own needs?

It is not sufficient that you think the child will benefit from, for example, structured practice in plurals. If he/she does not feel motivated to learn them then learning will, at best, be very inefficient.

Self-confidence and Anxiety

Language learning is often regarded as primarily a cognitive task, with little attention paid to affective factors in determining how quickly language skills will develop. Research over the last twenty years is making it increasingly clear that negative attitudes and stereotypes towards other ethnolinguistic groups can interfere with the motivation to learn their languages (Giles and St. Clair, 1979). It is also true that positive and friendly attitudes to school, and parental influences may have an important effect on progress (Ashby *et al*, 1970). Similarly, the teacher's attitudes to the culture and language of the learner will be picked up by the child. It is likely that pupil's perceived rejection, by teachers or school, of their culture and home language will have detrimental effects on their acquisition of English. Further, learning another language, which may be used more than the mother tongue, can pose a threat to self-concept and cultural identity which can then interfere with the learning of the new language.

For really efficient learning to take place, it is essential that the child (or adult, for that matter):

— feels secure and accepted;
— feels he/she will be judged fairly, with due allowance being made for imperfect English;
— feels confident of understanding and of being understood;
— has the chance to practise and try things out in a non-threatening situation (so DON'T keep interrupting to correct 'mistakes' — DO wait patiently for an answer or say 'don't worry, I'll wait'). This could involve working in pairs or small groups to reduce anxiety, promote cooperation and provide more practice than in a whole class. It could also work in large (and therefore safe) groups for activities like singing or stories (Pepitone, 1985).

Linguistic and Related Factors

Research into second language acquisition suggests that different people have different styles of learning, so teachers must be able to teach in several different ways. Ventriglia (1982, cited by Chamot) has, for example, proposed three basic styles used by second language learners.

Beaders, who learn individual words first, then combine them.
Braiders, who learn in chunks or phrases.
Orchestrators who start by listening a lot to sounds and intonations and gradually build up an understanding.

It is increasingly accepted that, for all but a small group of students who are inclined to reflect on language learning, most language is 'acquired' rather than 'learned' (Krashen, 1978). It follows that the important factors will be:

Figure 4:   *Linguistic and related factors*

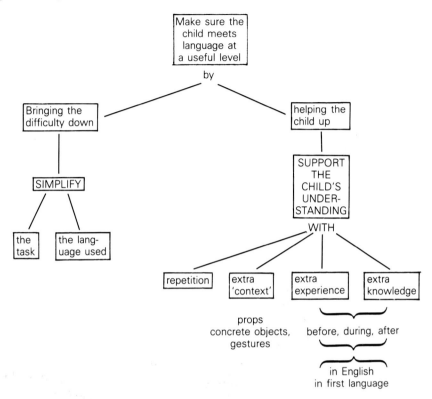

—hearing language that is a little above the student's current level, and

—analyzing meaning rather than structure.

It will not normally be helpful to correct errors systematically, or teach formal grammar.

Instead, teachers should respond to the intended meanings that children try to communicate, and should themselves provide a model of language that is natural, meaningful and useful to the children. It will be necessary to bring in other speakers with different styles and vocabularies. The teacher will need to arrange for the child to have some language input a little above his/her current level, some that is just at that level (for practice and confidence-boosting), and some period of rest, silence or non-verbal activity (since working in a new language is more tiring than using the first language).

There are a number of ways in which the effective level of language difficulties can be reduced by the teacher, and these are summarized in figure 4.

(i) *Repetition* — Language that is heard, read or written for the third or fourth time is easier to take in and more likely to stick, but it is not necessary to make great use of unnaturally repetitive exercises. There is plenty of natural repetition in school. For older children, the regular activities of the science, PE or games class, or of assembly and form period provide examples, while for younger learners there is a lot of potential in songs, stories, rhymes, games, as well as in giving out the milk, doing surveys, collecting in books. Collaborative learning allows all children to be useful as models. There are many opportunities but they call for thoughtful teacher intervention if they are to be fully exploited (Pepitone, *op. cit.*).

(ii) *Support from context (in its widest sense)* — This could, for example, involve an emphasis on practical activities using real objects, or provision of extra materials and visual aids to the second language learners within an ordinary lesson. It would involve more use of gestures and demonstrations by the teacher.

(iii) *Pace and preparation* — It is often possible to lower the effective rate at which material is presented by giving older ESL students notes, diagrams and vocabulary lists before the main lesson. In reading, the students control the pace and the number of repetitions, while in listening to a teacher 'live' they can only try to follow as best they can. Similarly, for younger children, it could be arranged for them to become acquainted with a topic before it is generally presented. They could have extra showings of a film, or attempts at a new game, beforehand, so they are better enabled to keep up with the other children later on. Bilingual books and materials are at last becoming much more readily available. (In many cases the most efficient way of giving advance preparation would be to use a bilingual teacher or assistant, but that, as we have already said, is another issue.)

Remember also that many children will meet English outside the class, and if they can be helped to make sense of this, and it is just above their current level, they will be enabled to learn. As far as literacy is concerned, the possibility of learning through the mother tongue rarely arises at present, through lack of sutiable resources and expertise. For young bilingual children, as for monolinguals learning to read English, we feel the important task of the teacher is to provide lively, engaging material which inevitably, many bilingual children will be slower getting started on reading when they have to learn in a second language, but there is no reason why they should not catch up. For older children, who arrive in their teens unable to read, a very different curriculum may have to be provided from that followed by their peers, particularly those on academic courses. (Though we know of individual bilingual teenagers literate in their own languages who have achieved strikingly good examination results soon after arriving in Britain).

Conclusion

Most children learning a second language are likely to take many years to acquire a full range of skills in spoken and written language. ESL learners will make their best progress only if the social, motivational and linguistic conditions are all satisfactory. It is now understood that this can rarely, if ever, be achieved through prolonged separation from mainstream schooling, and it is now an urgent task to increase the support given to ESL learner's linguistic and psychological development within ordinary classrooms. This will need a more coherently planned language curriculum from nursery through to secondary school. It will require a careful analysis of the ESL support necessary in each class, taking into consideration the language demands of the tasks as well as the linguistic competence, social skills and cultural backgrounds of the pupils. The principles outlined in this chapter should be employed, to ensure that bilingual learners whose English still needs support can nevertheless work in intellectually stimulating classrooms and experience academic and social success.

It is not suggested that all children should be thrust straight into mainstream classrooms whatever their linguistic and cultural background. In some circumstances centres may have an important role in introducing some children to the cultural expectations of their new situation, and provide them with a secure environment in which to develop their self-confidence and to reach the stage where they have the necessary motivation and understanding of the system to succeed in a mainstream classroom. In these cases placement in a centre would be for a few weeks or months rather than the much longer time normally associated with language centres.

It is clear that the main contribution of language specialists must be through working with, and alongside, mainstream colleagues, deepening their understanding of language growth and developing appropriate materials and strategies. The place for most of this work is the mainstream classroom.

References

ASHBY, B., MORRISON, A. and BUTCHER, H.J. (1970) 'The abilities and attainments of immigrant children', *Research in Education*, 4, pp 73–80.

BARNES, D. (1976) *From Communication to Curriculum*, Harmondsworth, Penguin.

CHAMOT, A. (1983) 'How to plan a transfer curriculum from bilingual to mainstream instruction'. *Focus*, 12, National Clearinghouse for Bilingual Education, USA.

CUMMINS, J. (1980) 'Psychological assessment of immigrant children: logic or intuition', *Journal of Multilingual and Multicultural Development*, 1, pp 97–111.

CUMMINS, J. (1981) 'Age on arrival and immigrant second language learning in Canada: a reassessment', *Applied Linguistics*, 2, pp 132–49.

CUMMINS, J. (1982) 'Tests, achievement and bilingual students', *Focus*, 9, National Clearinghouse for Bilingual Education, USA

DONALDSON, M. (1978) *Children's Minds*, Glasgow, Fontana.

ESSEN, J. and GHODSIAN, M. (1979) 'The children of immigrants: School performance', *New Community*, 1, 3, pp 422–9.

GILES, H. and ST. CLAIR, R. (1979) *Language and Social Psychology*, Oxford, Blackwell.

GOLDMAN, R. (1973) 'Education and immigrants', in WATSON P. (Ed) *Psychology and Race Education*, Harmondsworth, Penguin.

HOULTON, D. and WILLEY, R. (1983) *Supporting Children's Bilingualism*, Schools Council Programme 4, York, Longmans.

KRASHEN, S. (1982) *Principles and Practice in Second Language Acquisition*, Oxford, Pergamon.

LITTLE, A. (1975) 'Performance of children from ethnic minority backgrounds in primary schools', *Oxford Review of Education*, 1, 2.

LITTLE, A. and WILLEY, R. (1981) *Multi-ethnic Education: The Way Forward*, Schools Council Pamphlet 18, London, Schools Council.

MABEY, C. (1981) 'Black British literacy: A study of reading attainment of London black children from 8 to 15 years', *Educational Research*, 23, 2, pp 83–95.

PEPITONE, E.A. (1985) 'Children in co-operation and competition'. In SLAVIN, R., SHARAN, S., KAGAN, S., HERTZ-LAZAROWITZ, R., WEBB, C. and SCHMUCK, R. (Eds) *Learning to Co-operate: Co-operating to Learn*, New York, Plenum.

TOMLINSON, S. (1980) 'Educational performance of ethnic minority children', *New Community*, 8, 3, pp 213–34.

WELLS, G. (1981) *Learning Through Interaction*, Cambridge, Cambridge University Press.

4   Racism Awareness: Training, Education and Accountability

Peter Pumfrey

Introduction

The chapter comprises three sections. The first illustrates the social reality of racism and considers its definition. This is followed by a discussion of the aims and objectives of Racism Awareness Training (RAT). Problems associated with the evaluation of the efficacy of RAT are then discussed. The chapter concludes with five recommendations concerning RAT.

The background from which I write is that of having been employed as a qualified teacher, a specialist in remedial education, educational psychologist, research worker and university lecturer. Most of my career has been spent working in large industrialized urban conurbations with multicultural populations. My interest in the field of racism in general and of RAT in particular originated in an involvement in work on the relative reading attainments of various ethnic groups in our schools. It was further developed by several years' experience as a member of the British Psychological Society's Standing Committee on Equal Opportunities.

The use of specific incidents to illustrate aspects of racism in Britain can be criticized as little more than a sensationalism that exploits the emotional susceptibilities of readers. The abbreviated nature of such reports can lead to the creation of a distorted picture of what is happening in British society. Alternatively, to present only a range of statistical analyses specifying the incidence of racist behaviour would fail to put psychological and sociological flesh on such statistical bones. Initially the personal reality of racism will be described by referring to recently documented accounts in the Manchester area. The legal situation will then be commented on.

Racism

Going shopping can be an ordeal. To avoid abuse, insults and intimidation the family is forced to use a taxi. Windows of the house are covered with meshlight to keep out missiles. The family has lived in fear for some six years. Those harassed may know their assailants but be so frightened of further violence that they may be unwilling to say anything officially. Even when complaints are made formally to the police their actions are seen, by many who claim to be the victims of racism, to be ineffective.

In the same city, an attempt to set fire to the house of a black family has been described. The wife and her children were inside at the time, petrified with fear. They were saved by the actions of a friend who arrived in time to prevent the bushes that had been stacked against the front door from being lit. The family left the property the next day.

The above two examples of the racial harassment that derives from racist attitudes are claimed to be part of a growing trend in the city in question.

> For our own City Housing Department states that the incidence of racial harassment reported on council estates has increased significantly since 1982, when records were first started. (Cairncross, 1985)

It is also reported that the number of incidents of racial harassment notified to the City Council Housing Department has increased from one per month to six per month over the last three years. A Race Relations Advisor in the Housing Department is quoted as saying:

> Racial harassment is happening on all Manchester council estates, and, make no mistake about it, it is becoming more organized ... And we can't begin to analyze what may be happening on private estates.

Optimists argue that such an increase reflects not an increase in racist activity but an enhanced willingness by victims to report such matters. In this field assertions often replace facts. Pessimists take a different view and perceive a deteriorating situation. The individuals in the two cases cited earlier would certainly be in the latter group.

It has also been suggested that pupils in some secondary schools are encouraged in racist attitudes and behaviours by extremist political groups. A recent statement of government policy utterly rejects such activity (Committee of Inquiry into the Education of Children for

Minority Ethnic Groups, 1985). Such a situation is unlikely to optimize the educational attainments of pupils from minority or majority groups.

Incidents of racist behaviour in education appear in the press with distressing regularity. Such publicized reports are likely to be but the tip of an iceberg. The stabbing and killing of a 13-year-old Asian boy at a Manchester secondary school in 1986 is a dramatic example. It has led to the setting up of an independent inquiry into allegations of racial violence. In February 1987 the chairperson of the City Council's Race Sub-committee was reported as saying:

> We are aware that racism exists throughout our society and
> our schools and therefore the inquiry must take account of this
> and make positive recommendations to deal with racism.

Some observers would question the validity of this analysis. Like every sociopolitical debate, it has an ideological character that is infrequently made explicit. Irrespective of ideology, no responsible citizen of any political hue would condone the aggression described above towards *any* member of the community. A key question is, 'What can be done to prevent racism wherever it occurs?'. It would be unfortunate, and possibly counterproductive, if anti-racism became identified with any one political grouping in society.

Readers will be well aware of the belief systems concerning racial differences and the historical/social contexts within which racism develops and is maintained. The catalogue will not be rehearsed here. We need to accept that the right to a non-racist society has con-commitent responsibilities for all groups and all individuals in our society. As John Donne said, 'No man is an island ...'. Nor can any group, irrespective of colour, creed or composition, be isolated from the main.

An appreciation of the nature of racism is essential if the aims, methods and efficacy of RAT are to be understood and subject to the critical scrutiny that any form of training requires.

According to the Runnymede Trust, the Commission for Racial Equality, the Division of Criminological and Legal Psychology of the British Psychological Society, and the Home Office respectively, racism is not a term which occurs in statute law in either England, Wales or Scotland. The law only deals with particular mainfestations of racism. The Race Relations Act (1976) makes it unlawful to discriminate on grounds of colour, race, nationality, or ethnic or national origins. The Act also makes incitement to racial hatred illegal. Such incitement is '... committed by any person who publishes or distributes written matter which is threatening, abusive or insulting, or when he uses in any public place or at any public meeting words which are threatening, abusive or insulting'. In the civil courts there have been libel cases where the use of the name 'racist' has been claimed to be defamatory. In 1984, the headteacher of a school in Wolverhampton successfully sued a member of the Indian Workers' Association who had called the headteacher a racist. In 1983, an individual, called a racist in an article that appeared in *The New Statesman*, was awarded damages. A case brought by an individual against *The Guardian* newspaper that allegations of racism published in it were libelous, was successful. The case is now going to the Court of Appeal. The law and the courts will continue to be involved in clarifying the meaning of the term racism. Section 71 of the Race Relations Act (1976) lays on local authorities a two-fold responsibility in connection with the services they provide. The first is to eliminate unlawful racial discrimination and the second is to provide equality of opportunity and good relations between persons of different racial groups.

Some workers draw a distinction between racialism and racism. The former refers to the explicit negative beliefs and attitudes, and to offensive and often violent behaviours, shown by individuals and groups to other different but ethnically identifiable individuals and groups. The publications and the policies of, for example, the National Front and the British Movement, have been quoted as examples. The verbal abuse that occurs and the graffiti to be found in many places, are others. It is argued that racism incorporates racialism, but is a broader concept as it includes practices and policies in public and private institutions involving often unconscious and unintentional effects as well as conscious and deliberate purposes. Racism '... summarizes all attitudes, procedures and social patterns whose effects (though not necessarily whose conscious intention) is to create and maintain the power, influence and well-being of white people at the expense of Asian and Afro-Caribbean people; and whose further function is simultaneously to limit the latter to the poorest life chances and living conditions, the most menial work, and the greatest likelihood of unemployment and under-employment' (Committee of Inquiry into the Education of Children from Ethnic Minority Groups, 1985, p. 369). The preceding statement comes from one local authority's evidence to the Swann Committee. It continues by identifying three components of racism: (a) power, participation and influence; (b) practices, procedures and customs; and (c) beliefs and attitudes. By contrasting the manifestations of (a), (b) and (c) in situations where racism and then equality and justice are respectively displayed, the importance of institutional racism is demonstrated.

Four major reasons are advanced for moving from a society permeated by racism to one exemplified by equality and justice. The first is that racism is morally wrong as it involves benefitting some groups to the disadvantage of others. Secondly, in society's long-term interests, the social unrest produced by racism is damaging to the fabric of society. Thirdly, racism distorts people's views of their own cultural history and identity. The fourth reason is that racism prevents groups within society learning from each other, enriching the common culture and cooperating for the benefit of all groups.

Local authorities, private sector employers and many other groups, are developing anti-racist policies. The impetus of the Swann Report represents one important educational contribution. The policies of the ILEA represent another. Irrespective of whether one agrees entirely with either of these or not, they cannot be ignored (Cohen and Cohen, 1986, section I).

The relation between prejudice and racism is important. The former refers to unfavourable opinions or feelings that are formed without prior knowledge or reason. Prejudice is learned through society's processes of socialization. It is not inherited. Both black and white groups can show prejudice.

Racism entails a combination of prejudice with powers to carry out practices, whether overt or covert, conscious or otherwise, that subordinate other individuals or groups. If it is true that black people in Britain have no power, it follows that they can be prejudiced but not racist.

Not everyone accepts that black people are institutionally powerless in our society. Not all accept that black citizens are necessarily non-racist. Commentators have observed that anti-racism can lead to a situation where it is possible to make a moral virtue out of denigrating and despising those views, opinions and beliefs one dislikes because they challenge the truth perceived by believers. The anti-racism lobby inevitably produces a reaction (Palmer, 1986).

The Chairman of the Commission for Racial Equality has written '... most writing on race and education is unbalanced and ill-tempered because it is conducted by people who believe racism is what other people are doing wrong, whereas it often lies in what they themselves are not doing right. Getting to grips with that is hard' (Newsam, 1986).

Concern has been shown by the government, by local authorities and by individuals about the phenomenon of racism. A range of legal and educational measures is being tried to reduce racism in Britain. Proposals for changing the Race Relations Act (1976) in 1987 are under active consideration by a number of groups including the Commission for Racial Equality. The complexity of the situation is such that *no* single approach is likely to resolve satisfactorily the issues involved. Recognition of the existence of the problems of racism and an understanding of its nature still remain the essential first steps in dealing with it constructively.

My personal opinion is that racism *does* exist in our society, that it is undesirable and that steps should be taken to eradicate it. I am also certain that to achieve this end requires a long-term and sustained educative process. In this context, education is not restricted to the formal processes identified with schools, but includes a far broader concept. There are strategies that can help. Handbooks are available (for example, Katz, 1983). An excellent account of the organization, methodology and evaluation of a Racism Awareness Workshop for Teachers held in Manchester provides *one* example of what has been done, made public, and can be built upon (Gledhill and Heffernan, 1984).

Britain is a multi-racial community. The possible causes and negative consequences of overt and covert, of individual and structural racism, have received considerable attention. Racism Awareness Training (hereinafter RAT) is seen as *one* means whereby, using a range of approaches, racism in our society might be minimized. How valid is this assumption?

To consider such issues, the Commission for Racial Equality convened a one-day seminar in October 1984 on RAT. The seminar focussed on two main themes. The first of these, part I, was the aims and objectives of RAT. The second, part II, was on evaluating the efficacy of RAT.

I took part in the seminar. A report of the proceedings has been published (Commission for Racial Equality, 1985). What follows are my personal reflections on the composition of the seminar and on the two major themes that were considered.

As a visitor from the north-west, I found the list of participants interesting. Participants from the Greater London area and the south-east outnumbered by 26:5 those from other areas. The reasons for the absence of participants from, for example, Bristol, Liverpool, Leeds and Nottingham were alluded to in passing. Whilst accepting that there was no requirement that the seminar be in any way representative of providers and 'consumers' of RAT, the limited sample of participants must have affected the range of opinions and comment expressed in both part I and part II of the meeting. Despite this limitation, the interchange of views was of value in making explicit some of the conflicting viewpoints among individuals committed to combatting racism in Britain.

The following comments link with the pattern of the seminar. Part I concerns the session on the 'Aims and Objectives of Racism Awareness Training' and part II bears on 'Evaluation'. The comments are all made in a personal capacity.

Part I — Aims and Objectives of RAT

The acronym 'RAT' includes the word 'training'. The distinction between 'training' and 'education' is important both in theory and in practice. The former is associated with experiences that are restricted, closed; the latter with ones emphasizing breadth and openness. I would prefer to see RAT become RAE (Racism Awareness Education). However, irrespective of the label given to the variety of activities currently identified as RAT, it is important to consider *why* RAT appears necessary (Gurnah, 1984).

RAT has developed in response to dissatisfactions with the means whereby economic, political and financial power and opportunity operate in our multicultural society. These dissatisfactions have been felt and commented on by members of *all* ethnic groups, but particularly by those groups who see themselves as victims. RAT is about changing individual and institutional attitudes and structures. The objectives include a more equitable distribution of power, status and opportunities in a multicultural society. Put simply (perhaps too simply), RAT is a response to tensions in a multicultural society between the 'haves' and the 'have nots'. It is not a new phenomenon.

If this point is not made explicit, we run the risk of misleading ourselves. If this suggestion is valid, the threat of RAT to groups favouring the status quo becomes clear. The issue of the means whereby awareness is raised then becomes important.

A central concern of RAT is for changes in individuals and society. The means by which changes are initiated and sustained are inextricably bound up with assumptions made concerning how an unsatisfactory situation *developed* and is *maintained*. These two considerations are not necessarily the same. Some advocates of an historico-economic-political theory of causality argue that capitalism is inevitably implicated in both. Put crudely, to be white and live in a capitalist society is, almost unavoidably, to be racist. To some participants at the seminar, it appeared that only those who appreciate and unreservedly accept the validity of this hypothesis, those who have escaped the pervasive influences of capitalism in maintaining the status quo, can see what is required in order to achieve change. Whilst accepting the importance of the 'black' experience of oppression in this context, other groups in society also experience discrimination and oppression. More tolerance of each others' contributions between providers of different styles of RAT would probably be helpful. Or is this being too idealistic?

The account by a worker in Sheffield headlined 'Black racists' suggests that there are huge gaps between the theory and practice of developing tolerance and acceptance between and within ethnic groups in a multicultural society. The assertion that 'Prejudice exists in everyone. Racism is one form of it. But it is not necessarily a matter of colour' merits more than passing consideration (Weller, 1985). The dangers of substituting slogans for thinking has so long a history that the perils should be well-recognized by now. 'Black is beautiful' and 'white is right' are equally suspect. We need to beware of the absolute certainty of dogmatists, irrespective of their provenance. Under the guise of the slogan there lies implicit but often unacknowledged special pleading by groups.

The subsequent public disassociation from Weller's views by members of the Anti-Racist Group of Sheffield's Adult Education Branch of the National Association of Teachers in Further and Higher Education (NATFHE) underlines the strength and diversity of opinions generated by the issues (letters, *Times Educational Supplement*, 3595, p. 14).

Because it is concerned with encouraging individual and institutional changes in sensitive fields, irrespective of the validity of *any* causal hypothesis, RAT is likely to be perceived as a threat by many institutions and individuals in this country. RAT aims to subvert racism. However, the notion that racism is the sole prerogative of any one group in our society denies the essentially intercultural nature of the tensions that lead to, and maintain, the beliefs and practices embodying racism. Minority groups, oppressed or otherwise, cannot remain uninvolved in the stereotyping, simplifications and polarization manifest in racism. The assertion that racism involves all groups is usually rejected on the grounds that the dynamics of power in our society have been ignored. As mentioned earlier, the reasoning is that if minority groups have no power to carry out policies and practices that adversely impinge on other groups, the former *cannot* be racist. The danger lies not in the element of validity in such a claim, but in the oversimplification that follows from its unquestioning acceptance as all that needs or can be said about the matter.

How should RAT leaders be selected? Do they require training in training? How can this be done and by whom? Or are such questions unimportant? These issues were not addressed at the seminar.

Can RAT effect changes by evolutionary approaches or are revolutionary methods necessary? In this respect, the comments made by participants at the seminar concerning the functions of 'self-confrontation' and 'confrontation' in RAT could, to advantage, be explicated. The methodologies of RAT are very important. Whilst not assuming that racist attitudes and racist behaviours are necessarily identical, a great deal is known about how such attitudes and behaviours develop, are maintained and can be changed (Sattow, 1982; Shaw *et al.*, 1987). Procedures whereby these attitudes and behaviours can be made resistant to change are also known. It is worrying that techniques advocated as necessary for change can lead to the opposite. The argument that polarization is unavoidable, indeed essential, to produce changes that reduce racism is questionable. The means and the ends involved must be consonant with one another.

In writing these comments I am well aware that the interpretations put on them depends, in part, on whether they chime or clash with the reader's experience and views. The same applies to all of us. My major concern is that individuals and groups should listen to each other, rather than reject out of hand other viewpoints, other analyses, other courses of action, other values. In this respect, empirical data must be collected, presented and considered as one means of making explicit the phenomena under review. We need to use both descriptive and inferrential statistics to inform this debate.

RAT trainers were divided concerning the aims, objectives and methods of training, except when these were stated in very general terms. Operationally defined objectives would be likely to identify the diversity of aims and objectives underlying the general aims and objectives of RAT. Most RAT trainers could agree with the unexceptional assertion that trainers must start with trainees 'where they are'.

Ideas on the racial/ethnic composition of groups and trainers, the experiences leading to enhanced self-awareness, the utility of confrontation as a technique and the training of the trainers, underlined different viewpoints held by participants on a range of central practical issues. Although interpretations would still differ, agreed definitions of different forms and modes of RAT (or, preferably, RAE) could reduce misunderstanding between groups whose work is based on the concept. At the very least, differences could be made clear so that their rational consideration is possible by all.

If RAT is to be more than a sop to political susceptibilities, it is essential that individuals who shape policies should experience RAT. The danger that RAT could harden the racist attitudes of some individuals or groups cannot be dismissed lightly. RAT providers seeking public financial support will need to be explicit concerning their assumptions, aims, objectives and methods. If a group sees the entire white society as racist, the battle to capture the hearts and minds of the majority is a daunting task.

The essential questions of 'How are RAT trainers selected?' and 'Who trains the RAT trainers?' were not adequately explored at the seminar. They should be. The field of RAT is complex. It is understandable that trainers should believe strongly in their particular approach. However, at this stage, for any *one* group to claim that its selection procedures for trainers, its analysis, aims, objectives and methods are the only valid ones, is logically untenable. Such an assertion manifests an absence of the tolerance that RAT seeks to develop. Of equal importance, such oversimplifications are likely to lead to disappointment. No single group or individual has a panacea for the problems of individual and institutional racism in Britain.

Part II — Evaluation of RAT

Course aims, objectives and methods of delivery for specified groups should be made explicit by all RAT trainers. In a democracy, public knowledge is of the essence. Any group unwilling to make public and open to debate its purposes and methods is likely to come under suspicion. It is NOT sufficient to say 'Come and join us and experience what we are doing'. Such an approach smacks of indoctrination rather than education. With no consensus on operationally defined objectives, the identification of 'good practice' is impossible.

The range of assessment techniques for appraising the efficacy of RAT is far more extensive than became apparent during the discussion at the seminar. Social scientists have developed an extensive array of techniques. To claim, as one group appeared to do, that the 'in-course' assessments used were 'different' and individually appropriate, was an important statement. However, no details were given, despite a request for them. We were left with only an assertion. If

RAT has led to developments in assessment methodology, this is an important matter on which further public information should be made available.

In common with many others, I have spent much of my professional (and personal) life trying to find out which educational techniques work at particular times with which individuals and groups in what circumstances. I recognize that acts of faith are necessary at times. I am also aware of the tautology expressed by the Greek physician Galen. In the absence of evidence to the contrary, it suggests a criticism of RAT in the UK.

> All who drink this remedy recover in a short time, except those whom it does not help, who all die and have no relief from any other medicine. Therefore it is obvious that it only fails in incurable cases.

The assertion that 'accountability' is a concept invoked by a hostile society as a means of frustrating RAT is, at best, suspect. We were informed that RAT in Britain has a longish track record. RAT course providers should be able to specify what is being achieved. As was remarked many years ago, 'Whatever exists, exists in some quantity and can, *in principle*, be measured'. This is a valid comment concerning the process and products of RAT training as of *any* other form of training. RAT trainers in other countries have presented evidence on the efficacy of their programmes. It is not unreasonable to ask that the same be done in the UK. What we need to do is to identify effective training procedures.

For example, a number of LEAs run racism awareness courses for teachers. It would be valuable to all involved in developing RAT if accounts of this work were published. Manchester LEA has run a series of Racism Awareness Workshops for Teachers. The course organizers have described the organization of such courses, the development of a group of trainers, the rationale and the aims of the workshops. They have also presented details of the programme and of its evaluation. Their article does not claim to present the solution to RAT but to describe their endeavours in such a way that both they and others can learn from them (Gledhill and Heffernan, 1984). Other RAT course organizers should be encouraged to do likewise for the benefit of all. We *all* need to know more about the range of techniques and strategies available for improving race relations and reducing racism (National Union of Teachers, 1983; Shaw *et al.*, 1987).

Conclusions

1 RAT should become RAE (Racism Awareness Education).
2 If it is to be effective, advocates must persuade citizens that what RAE offers is of value to society in general.
3 There are many ways of combating racism. Tolerance by RAE course providers of a variety of approaches would probably be mutually beneficial in achieving the general aims and objectives that they have in common.
4 RAE course providers should publish accounts of their work.
5 Both the formative (process) and summative (outcomes) aspects of RAE should be described and evaluated.

References

CAIRNCROSS, C. (1985) 'Racial harassment', *The Manchester Magazine*, 6, pp. 10–11.
COHEN, L. and COHEN, A. (Eds) (1986) *Multicultural Education: A Sourcebook for Teachers*, London, Harper Education Series.
COMMISSION FOR RACIAL EQUALITY (1985) *A Report on the Seminar on Racism Awareness Training held on 31 October 1984.* London, Commission for Racial Equality.
COMMITTEE OF INQUIRY INTO THE EDUCATION OF CHILDREN FROM ETHNIC MINORITY GROUPS (1985) *Education for All,* (Swann Report) Cmnd. 9453, London, HMSO.
GLEDHILL, M. and HEFFERNAN, M. (1984) 'Racism awareness workshops for teachers', *Educational and Child Psychology*, 1, 1, pp 46–59.
GURNAH, A. (1984) 'The politics of racism awareness training', *Critical Social Policy*, 10, pp 6–20.
KATZ, J.H. (1983) *White Awareness: Handbook for Anti-racism*, Norman, OK, University of Oklahoma Press.
NATIONAL UNION OF TEACHERS (1983) *Racism Awareness Workshop*, Stoke Rochford Hall, NUT.
NEWSAM, P. (1986) 'Beating bias', *Times Educational Supplement* 27 June, p. 80.
OPEN UNIVERSITY (1983) *Racism in Workplace and Community*, Milton Keynes, Open University Press.
PALMER, F. (Ed) (1986) *Anti-racism: An Assault on Education and Value*, London, Sherwood Press.
SATTOW, A. (1982) 'Racism awareness training: Training to make a difference', in OHRI, B.M. and CURNO (Eds) *Community Work and Racism*, London, Routledge and Regan Paul, pp 34–42.
SHAW, J., NORDLIE, d P.G. and SHAPIRO, R.M. (Eds) (1987) *Strategies for Improving Race Relations: The Anglo-American Experience*, Manchester, Manchester University Press.

SWANN, M. (1985) *Education for All: A Brief Guide to the Main Issues of the Report*, London, HMSO.
WELLER, M. (1985) 'Black racists', *Times Educational Supplement*, 3950, 19 April, p. 18.

5   The Swann Report and Ethnic Minority Attainment

Bhikhu Parekh

The Swann Report is a complex and uneven document (Committee of Inquiry into the Education of Children from Ethnic Minority Groups, 1985). In some respects it rises above the current consensus and breaks new ground, whereas in others it is rather pedestrian and conservative. I shall begin by pointing to some of its limitations, and then turn to what seems to me to be its major contribution.

The Report has several limitations. First, it lacks a clear conception of its problematic. Like the earlier Rampton Report (Committee of Enquiry into the Education of Children from Ethnic Minority Groups, 1981), it establishes the fact that the West Indian children grossly underachieve in British schools. It shows that in 1978–79, in all CSE and GCE 'O' level examinations, only 3 per cent of West Indian children in the five LEAs surveyed obtained five or more higher grades, compared with 17 per cent of Asians, and 16 per cent of all other school leavers in these LEAs and 21 per cent in England as a whole. It shows also that during the three years since its first survey, the educational achievements of the West Indian children showed remarkable improvement. Their figure rose to 6 per cent, whereas the other three only rose to 17, 19 and 23 per cent respectively.

At the GCE 'A' level in 1978–79, only 2 per cent of the West Indian children gained one or more passes compared with 12 per cent Asians, 12 per cent other school leavers in the five LEAs surveyed and 13 per cent in England as a whole. Three years later, the West Indian percentage had risen to 5, whereas the others only rose to 13, 13 and 14 respectively.

The Report thus had to explain first, the West Indian children's underachievement and second, their remarkable improvement between 1978–79 and 1981–82. The two explanations are closely related for the explanation of the second throws light on the factors responsible for the first. For reasons difficult to understand, the Report only concentrates on the former. In so doing, it obscures the important and heartening fact that West Indian children's performance showed dramatic improvement during a short span of three years. Further, by failing to explore what external factors could have changed during the brief period, it remains unable to explain their underachievement. Their family structure, temperament and 'natural endowments' obviously could not have undergone a change in such a short period. The attitudes and expectations of the teachers could have, especially as the Rampton Report had laid so much emphasis on them, and so also perhaps the West Indian parents' and children's ability to cope with their problems and the remarkable growth of supplementary schools. It is also likely that other factors might have been at work for some time and begun to show their results during the three-year period. Whatever the explanation, the Report missed an important opportunity and presented a one-sided picture.

Second, the Report shows considerable vacillation in explaining the educational underachievement of West Indian children. It stresses the disturbing incidence of racism both in society at large and in the schools. However, it makes the opposite mistake to Rampton's. While the latter tended to be a little too sweeping, the Swann Report adds so many qualifications and so often calls for yet more research, some of which it could itself have commissioned, that its emphasis on racism remains tentative and half-hearted.

Third, the Report is grossly unfair to the Asians. Since the Rampton Committee was specifically concerned with the West Indian children, the Swann Committee was expected and indeed required by the initial terms of reference to concentrate on the other ethnic minority children. It did not do so, evidently with the full cooperation of its Asian members. As a result it not only did injustice to them, but also to the West Indian children whom it could not study in a comparative perspective. Furthermore, it presented the Asian children as high achievers, and ignored the obvious fact that the Asian community consists of several sub-communities with widely differing levels of educational achievement. The Indian children as a rule tend to achieve better than their Pakistani counterparts, whereas the Bangladeshi children perform little better than the West Indian. The high Indian average is largely a result of the fact that the Indians have a higher than average proportion of the middle classes whose children achieve better than the national average, and conceals the fact that the educational performance of their working class compatriots falls far below the national average. Compared to 7 per cent of the whites, 10 per cent of the Indians and about 6 per cent of Pakistanis and Bangladeshis belong to the professional classes. Whereas 9 per cent of the white males and 4 per cent white females have university degrees or professional qualifications, the corresponding figures among the Indians are 15 and 8 per cent respectively. All this means that the data relating to the educational achievements of Asian children need to be read with much greater care than that displayed by the Swann Report.

Fourth, the Report's treatment of the place of ethnic minority languages in our schools is unimaginative, unfair and self-contra-dictory. It says that the ethnic minorities should be not only free but positively assisted to preserve their identities and that this involves preserving their languages, yet it peremptorily dismisses the case for teaching them in primary schools. It ignores the large body of research on the educational value of bilingualism, misrepresents the case for teaching English through the medium of the community languages for at least the first year or two, and fails to appreciate that the very arguments it advances for offering these languages in secondary schools requires them to be offered in primary schools as well. Indeed, if the linguistic skills the ethnic minority children initially bring with them to the schools are suppressed or not treated with respect, it is not clear what motives they could have to study them in the secondary schools.

Fifth, the report is deeply ambiguous in its attitude to the current controversy between multicultural and anti-racist education, and points in two different directions. Its main text is articulated in the langu-age of multicultural education whereas its appendices gesture in the direction of anti-racist education. Perhaps such a compromise was politically necessary to secure the agreement of the Committee. Whatever the reasons the Report lacks theoretical clarity on this crucial question. It does not notice that the debate between the two views rests on misunderstanding and is not to be found in the United States, Australia and Canada where it is taken for granted that multicultural education is impotent without an anti-racist thrust, and anti-racist education is educationally misdirected and fragile unless grounded in a multicultural perspective. It is a pity that a major government Report did not undertake a detailed analysis of the debate, examine the assumptions and educational philosophies of the warring but essentially complementary theories, and work out a perspective incorporating their valid insights and avoiding their ideological exaggerations.

Finally, although the Report is underpinned by a sincere commitment to pluralism, it neither clearly defines its nature and implications nor comes to grips with the attendant problems. As it understands pluralism, the latter steers clear of assimilation or obliteration of ethnic identities on the one hand, and separatism or intensification of the identities on the other, and entails their preservation within a framework of shared values. Since the issue is of considerable importance, the Report's relevant remarks deserve to be quoted in full.

We consider that a multiracial society such as ours would in fact function most effectively and harmoniously on the basis of pluralism which enables, expects and encourages members of all ethnic groups, both minority and majority, to participate fully in shaping the society as a whole within a framework of commonly accepted values, practices and procedures, whilst also allowing and, where necessary, assisting the ethnic minority communities in maintaining their distinct ethnic identities within this common framework. Clearly the balance between the shared common identity of society as a whole and the distinct identities of different ethnic groups is crucial in establishing and maintaining a pluralist society, and it must be recognized that such a society places obligations on both the minority and majority groups within it, if it is to offer them all a full range of benefits and opportunities. In a democratic pluralist society, we believe all members of that society, regardless of ethnic orgin, have an obligation to abide by the current laws of the country and to seek to change them only through peaceful and democratic means, but there is also an obligation on government to ensure equal treatment and protection by the law for members of all groups, together with equality of access to education and employment, equal freedom and opportunity to participate fully in social and political life, both locally and nationally, equal freedom of cultural expression and equal freedom of conscience for all. The ethnic majority community in a truly pluralist society cannot expect to remain untouched and unchanged by the presence of ethnic minority groups — indeed the concept of pluralism implies seeing the very diversity of such a society, in terms for example of the range of religious experience and the variety of languages and language forms, as an enrichment of the experience of all those within it. Similarly, however, the ethnic minority communities cannot in practice preserve all elements of their cultures and lifestyles unchanged and in their entirety — indeed if they were to wish to do so it would in many cases be impossible for them then to take on the shared values of the wider pluralist society. In order to retain their identities when faced with the pervasive influences of the lifestyle of the majority community, ethnic minority groups must nevertheless be free within the democratic framework to maintain those elements which they themselves consider to be the most essential to their sense of ethnic identity — whether these take the form of adherence to a particular religious faith or the maintenance of their own language for use within the home and their ethnic community — without fear of prejudice or persecution by other groups. It is important to emphasize here free choice for individuals, so that all may move and develop as they wish within the structure of the pluralist society. We would thus regard a democratic pluralist society as seeking to achieve a balance between, on the one hand, the maintenance and active support of the essential elements of the cultures and lifestyles of all the ethnic groups within it, and, on the other, the acceptance by all groups of a set of shared values distinctive of the society as a whole. This then is our view of a genuinely pluralist society, as both socially cohesive and culturally diverse.

The remarks just quoted point in so many different directions that one is not quite sure what they mean and imply. First, we are told that Britain is a *plural* society in the sense of consisting of different races and ethnic groups. We are also told that it is a *pluralist* society in the sense of welcoming and being committed to the preservation of its plural nature, a very different proposition for which little evidence is given. As if realizing that, although plural, Britain perhaps is not a pluralist society, the Report observes that it *ought* to be one, but its arguments are not clearly stated and defended.

Second, the Report remains delightfully vague about the nature of pluralism. It argues that since Britain is a *plural* even pluralist society, it should allow and even assist the ethnic minorities to preserve their identities. As a long established and internally coherent society, it also has a 'common identity' which it has a right and a duty to preserve. The Report therefore contends that it is 'crucial' to strike a 'balance' between the common British and the separate ethnic identities. Since this way of stating the problem is highly abstract and essentially mistaken we should not be surprised at its failure to deal with it.

Although the concept of identity is extremely problematic, the Report more or less takes it for granted and equates it with essence. It may perhaps make some sense when applied to an individual, but it is doubtful if it can be applied to groups, especially such large, fluid and abstract groups as states. The Report says that Britain's identity consists in 'commonly accepted values, practices and procedures', but does not say what they are beyond pointing to its democratic structure of government. Elsewhere it talks of 'common aims, attributes and values' and 'fundamental principles', but again gives them no concrete content.

The same problem occurs at the level of the ethnic minorities. The Report says that they 'must ... be free ... to maintain those elements which they themselves consider to be the most essential to their sense of ethnic identity', and suggests that these might include religion or language. It does not appreciate that members of an ethnic minority might stress different elements and greatly disagree in their definitions of its identity. More importantly, it does not recognize that even when an ethnic minority is agreed about the constitutive elements of its identity, these might conflict with the values central to British national identity. Some fundamentalist Muslims might wish to withdraw their daughters at the age of 15, demand polygamy and easy divorces, be opposed to alimony or ask for an official recognition of their traditional system of civil and criminal law. The Report gives little guidance about how we should deal with such cases. Again, it advocates pluralism on the ground that, among other things, it expands the area of individual choice. This is strange, for pluralism is centred around organized groups and not individuals, is concerned to preserve the former's unity and identity not the latter's liberty, and could prove detrimental to individual freedom and choice.

Despite these and other weaknesses, the Swann Report is an important document. It makes a powerful case for multicultural education, has many sensible things to say on education as a preparation for life, teacher training and the lines along which the structure and organization of the school need to be altered. Its greatest contribution lies in the way it approaches the underachievement of ethnic minority children. The problems of ethnic minority children had hitherto been discussed in isolation from mainstream education. The Report places them at its very centre, and argues that the problems of the ethnic minority children are tied up with and cannot be solved without changing the basic character of mainstream education. It links the two by means of the following four theses.

First, the ethnic minority children, especially the West Indians, grossly underachieve in British schools. Second, racism in British society in general and the schools in particular is one of the most important reasons for this. Third, racism can be countered by ensuring that the white children in our schools are educated in a non-racist manner. The future teachers, educational administrators, managers and political leaders will tend to come from the ranks of the children currently studying in all white schools. And therefore, if one of the root causes of ethnic minority children's underachievement is to be removed, white children must be given non-racist education. Fourth, multicultural education, which is equated in the Report with non-racist education, is therefore meant not just or even primarily for the ethnic minority children but for all, especially the white children. Hence, the title of the report, *Education for All*.

Consider the implications of these four propositions lying at the very heart of the Report. They imply that the future of ethnic minority children is intimately bound up with that of their white counterparts. Unless the latter are given better or non-racist education, the problems of the ethnic minority children will continue. The ethnic minority *have* problems but are not themselves *a problem*; rather, white racism *is* a problem. The basic thesis of the report, contained in these four propositions, implies further that the school cannot and should not remain neutral in racial matters. Since it is concerned with good or non-racist education for all its children, and since it is concerned also with the underachievement of its ethnic minority children for which white racism is largely responsible, the school must take on the task of eradicating racism. It should not passively reflect society; it must actively seek to change the attitudes of its future citizens within the limits of its power. This is a radical view of the nature and role of the school, which no other report had ever before advanced. Part of the credit for the ability of the Swann Report to go thus far must go to the Rampton Report which had done much of the required spadework and so formulated the problematic that its successor had no other option but to move in an educationally and racially radical direction. The Rampton Report had asked the right questions, and these dictated the direction in which their answers had to be explored. In this regard, the Swann Report remains firmly within the Ramptonian framework.

The Swann Report's great contribution, then, lies in giving the educational debate in Britain a new direction. Thanks to it, a new consensus is beginning to emerge, and the debate is beginning to acquire a new depth and dimension. Not just the schools with ethnic minority concentrations but *all* schools are now put under the microscope and drawn into the national debate. The Swann Report proposes 'Education for All', and from now onwards every school, including the all-white school, must show why it should not follow the report's lead, radically examine its structure, practices and curriculum, and ensure that its children receive non-racist education. Racism which, like sex, has so far been considered too respectable a subject to be discussed in polite company is now placed on the agenda of the national debate.

While conveying a radical message, the Report takes care to legitimize it in terms of the central values of British society. Most radicals fail to appreciate that every society has a specific conception of itself, a certain set of values which it regards as its unique historical achievement and in harmony with which it hopes to act and live. Its members *define* themselves and their identity in terms of these values. Their self-respect and sanity are tied up with their adherence to them, and they feel that they cannot respect themselves and avoid guilt, remorse and even self-hatred, if they cannot convince themselves that their actions, at least to some degree, conform to them. Even if a society's conception of itself, its view of what it means to be an Englishman, an American or a Frenchman, is deeply ideological, subserves the interests of the dominant class and is a form of false consciousness, it *is* sincerely held by the bulk of its members. Their actions are ultimately grounded in or at least articulated and justified in terms of it, and they simply cannot be influenced unless one articulates one's appeal in terms of their central values. Men are not abstract and ahistorical beings living by ahistorical principles. They *are* and perceive themselves as constituted in a specific manner, have specific conceptions of who they are and what kind of human beings they wish to be. Anyone interested in changing their behaviour must of necessity take their self-perception as his inescapable starting point.

In this sense every radical message has a conservative dimension. It starts, and must start, with the prevailing system of values, and show that, far from violating or subverting them, it only seeks to extend them in new but acceptable directions. In other words, a radical message only succeeds when it presents itself as the fulfilment of long-established and deeply cherished values. This is indeed what *persuasion* means. A radical who flaunts high sounding but abstract and irrelevant principles and lets loose a spate of denunciations may satisfy his nervous conscience or impress his restless constituents, but achieves nothing. His *rhetoric* does not relate to his society's values, and is inherently incapable of *persuading* its members.

The Swann Report avoids the familiar mistake of the ahistorical radical. It connects up its basic plea for non-racist education with the central values of British society at large and the British educational system in particular. It argues that, since education in the British view aims to *realize the child's potential*, society must do something about the gross underachievement of its ethnic minority children. It argues that since British society values *equality of opportunity and fairness*, it cannot deny them to these children. It argues, again, that *good or liberal education* as the British have always understood it involves cultivating such values as intellectual curiosity, respect for other men and their cultures and a regard for truth and objectivity, and that it is precisely these values that the British educational system does not adequately cultivate. What it teaches, how it teaches, the books it uses, the as- sumptions the teachers make, the way it presents other societies — all these perpetuate the old imperial stereotypes about the rest of the world, especially the Blacks, and reinforce racism. Much of what goes on in British schools is, therefore, simply not *good* or *liberal* education, and ought to be changed. In these and other ways the report turns the moral weapons of the system against itself, highlights its contradic- tions and demands that, if British society is really *sincere* about its values, it *must* adopt the proposed education for all. The Report did not push the argument as far as one would have liked, and remained more conservative than was justified. The point, however, remains that it has adopted the right strategy, and articulated its central con- cerns in a manner that British society cannot dismiss as 'irrelevant', 'foreign' or 'Marxist'.

It is in this context that Lord Swann's much-criticized guide to the Report should be seen (Swann, 1985). It does not claim to be a summary of, and is not therefore required to be faithful to the Report. It is what its title says, a guide. Read as such, it is a remarkable document. Michael Swann is an old-fashioned liberal. The vocabulary of race does not come easily to him. And indeed, by upbringing, temperament and a long and cloistered academic life, he is perhaps unequipped to deal with the racial question. One could see this in his early months as Chairman of the Committee. Over time he was exposed to the problems of the ethnic minority children. He began to study both the experiential and research evidence, and started to appreciate the harsh reality of the school. Slowly he began to change, modify his earlier perceptions and to appreciate the extent and impact of racism both in society at large and in the school. In the end he felt sufficiently convinced to subscribe to the basic propositions listed earlier and append his signature to the report. The guide tells the story of his transformation, the story of a sensitive, respectable, upper-class English academic gradually feeling compelled by the logic of evidence, to come round to the view that the ethnic minority children are capable of achieving far more than they do at present, that their potential is being stifled, and that racial discrimination in society at large, low teacher expectations and demeaning stereotypes are largely responsible for this. What has happened to one man can also happen to others. Therein lies the hope for the future.

References

COMMITTEE OF INQUIRY INTO THE EDUCATION OF CHILDREN FROM ETHNIC MINORITY GROUPS (1981) *West Indian Children in Our Schools.* (Rampton Report). Cmnd. 8273 London, HMSO.

COMMITTEE OF INQUIRY INTO THE EDUCATION OF CHILDREN FROM ETHNIC MINORITY GROUPS (1985) *Education for All*, (Swann Report). Cmnd. 9453 London, HMSO.

SWANN, M. (1985) *Education for All: A Brief guide to the Main Issues of the Report*, London, HMSO.

6   Policies and Promising Practices
       in Education

Peter Newsam

Many commentators believe that 'the most significant event of 1985 was the publication of the Swann Report, *Education For All* (Committee of Inquiry into the Education of Children from Ethnic Minority Group, 1985).' To this statement I reply 'Well was it?' For if it was, the second most significant must have been the fact that the Report has been almost entirely ignored by the government, except that the then Secretary of State (Sir Keith Joseph), within three days of the Report's publication, said a number of things that he was *not* going do do. One of them was to offer mandatory grants for access courses to higher education. The Swann Report said this was something that could be done quickly and relatively inexpensively to improve access from the black community to teaching and other professions. Anyhow, there was an immediate, unfavourable, answer on that. On the other hand, there has been sustained dithering about, for example, improving the number and promotional prospects of teachers from ethnic minorities.

Let me begin with a personal view of what is happening. If one is talking about racial matters, education is the hardest of all the issues to deal with. If one is talking about employment, what is going on in employment, what is the MSC doing or not doing and so on. These issues may be intractable but at least it is possible to see what one ought to be doing and to find out whether it has been done. You can find out whether in fact people *have* got on to certain MSC courses; you can find out whether they are employed in certain sorts of jobs and, if something is going wrong, do something about it and know when you have done it.

Details from a Commission for Racial Equality factsheet are presented as an appendix to this chapter in support of these assertions. The first four of the six fields specified in the factsheet demonstrate the extent and nature of discrimination in employment and training. The remaining two show vividly, at three different levels of educational qualification, that young people from ethnic minority backgrounds are less likely to find post-YTS employment than similarly qualified white leavers.

In education, however, there is a fundamental uncertainty. It is, in principle, less easy to be sure about what one is trying to do and, therefore, whether one has moved in the right direction or not. Furthermore, if one is talking about education for all, the issues are far wider than those relating to race or ethnic difference. We are not dealing with a fundamentally equitable education system from which ethnic groups happen to be excluded. If it were as simple as that, the whole thing would be easier to deal with. But we have had, just recently, a powerful reassertion from the government of the notion of hierarchy in our society in the way that the education system is to operate. This is a much wider issue than anything Swann's Committee dealt with.

That brings me to my first main point. In dealing with a complex issue like education, it is convenient to take a particular viewpoint. If one is teaching in the classroom, that view will relate to what can be done within that classroom. As a head, one has a different perspective. Again, as an administrator looking from the outside, rubbing one's nose up against the windows of the education system if you like, there is yet another perspective.

My viewpoint today will be that from the Commission for Racial Equality (CRE). The Commission is a statutory body with statutory functions, so I have to relate the way the law functions to what is happening in education.

Looking at Swann, what is implied in that perspective? First, bearing in mind our own functions as a Commission, we have to consider what is being done to reduce the levels of racial discrimination in this country. Second, we have to look at what is being done to provide equal opportunities for all. Third, what stage have we reached in improving relationships between different groups of people in this country?

There is a logical connection between these three perspectives to the Commission's work; and a human priority to it also. Getting rid of racial discrimination underlies the whole issue of improving relationships. That is easily explicable in human terms. It would be impossible for us in a large gathering to be friendly, for example, if the majority of us had decided that the front row should spend the morning standing up, and then, at lunchtime, said to the front row 'let's make up and be friends'. There would be strong resistance from those who had been discriminated against by the majority. They would say, 'Before you deal with this matter of being friendly, justify your treatment of us. Until that is done, we do not believe in your offer of friendship'. It is impossible to build good relationships where there remains a powerful sense of injustice. That is where, as a Commission, we start and, where the education system has also to start.

The first question that we are concerned with in the Commission is how to reduce the levels of racial discrimination within the school system or anywhere else. To do that one has to be clear about the nature of the discrimination that occurs in school systems and elsewhere. The easiest form of discrimination to deal with is direct: straightforwardly treating one person or set of people less favourably than others on racial grounds. An example of direct racial discrimination is the form of stereotyping that we have all encountered. Stereotyping need not be hostile in intent but, to be discriminatory, must be harmful in effect. Consider a teacher talking to a black youngster in a school and negotiating for some homework, rather than insisting when insistence was necessary. The effect might be to reduce that youngster's performance, but the reason for the teacher's behaviour, the stereotype, might be that 'black youngsters flare up if you try to be strict'.

Direct discrimination, whether deliberately hostile or otherwise, is always intended so, in that sense, it is easy to get at.

Indirect discrimination, the second form of discrimination the law recognizes, is very different. Indirect discrimination is a matter of operating systems, applying rules or conditions, which have the effect, whether intended or not, of disproportionately disadvantaging one particular group in ways which cannot be justified. The Swann Committee was not forthright on the subject of indirect discrimination, although they quoted a group called ACER, on page 183, which analyzed the systematic things that go on in school which can discriminate against people from particular groups. Take the case of the way pupils are suspended from attendance at school. An education authority may have a suspension system which applies to all children and let us suppose that there is no evil or racial motive in that suspension system whatever. But the fact is that black youngsters may end up being suspended in greater numbers and for longer periods than others. Why? Suppose the school has a system whereby it says that, before a pupil comes back into school after suspension, the parents have to come to school to meet the teacher concerned or the head teacher. Now suppose the meetings are always arranged in the afternoon, at 4.30 pm. In a city like London, where there are a number of single-parent families and where many women are out working, a disproportionately large number of black mothers may simply not be allowed away from their work at that time of the day. It may take them a fortnight or three weeks longer to get into the school than other people who are not in that position. So, quite unintentionally, the system that has been adopted to deal with suspension has the effect of ensuring that black youngsters are out of school for longer periods than others. That is a form of indirect discrimination. The systems that we operate in our schools, running all the way through suspension to the way pupils are put in for certain sorts of examination, are shot through with problems of that kind.

Having clarified the nature of racial discrimination, the second task is to try and get rid of it. This is not a matter for neutrality. It has certainly been a worry to me, working my way through the local educational authorities of this country, particularly in areas where there are very few young people from the ethnic minorities, that people believe discrimination is one of those things that one might wish to deal with or decide not to take on. As you know, the prime message of Swann, embodied in its title *Education for All*, is that we are educating all people, not just one group of people, for life in a changed, multiethnic society. Getting rid of discrimination and iden-tifying what it is and how to deal with it is not a matter for neutrality. Discrimination is straightforwardly against the law. It is as much against the law as stealing. It must therefore be right that the funda-mental notion of justice, which has underpinned education since Plato, who was hardly a liberal, should actively be promoted in school. Conversely, as racial discrimination is a particular form of injustice, it must be right to be teaching against that. If you wish to call that teaching anti-racist, well and good.

The third thing I want to say is that, just as tackling dis-crimination is the best way of improving relationships, so too is the fact that the teaching involved must be applied to all schools. That is what education for all, Swann's title, implies. Injustice is an indivisible notion. It is as important to be clear about that in Cornwall as it is in the middle of London or Bradford. Many of the hate letters we get in the Commission come from places where there are few people from any minority group. Attitudes are worse in those areas than they are in the cities and, unfortunately, that is true of teachers as well as others.

The fourth point is that, teaching is not just a matter of instruc-tion. A sensible response to a multi-ethnic society means that materials used in school have to be relevant to what is being taught. This is not a matter of censorship; it is a matter of common sense. When we moved to a decimal system in this country we removed from our books a lot of references to rods, poles and perches and the age-old measurements we had used. Similarly, there have been changes in the political composition of the world in the last forty years. The maps have changed colour accordingly. We do not go on using the atlases we had in the 1930s. So what is being suggested now is that we ensure the materials we use are appropriate to the world and political setting within which we live. We must live in the present to prepare for the future.

Fifth, the individual flair of a teacher, on which so much excitement for individual pupils depends, is not a sufficient response to the issues raised by education in a multiracial society. There needs to be a systematic shift of thinking and practice. This means that the institution as a whole, the school or college, has to rethink and, so far as possible unitedly, determine the direction in which it needs to go.

Let me now move on to the Commission's concern with equal opportunities. As I have hinted earlier, there is not a great deal that can be done within the school system to straighten out the structural, economic or social problems in the society surrounding the schools. There is a role, however limited, in preparing the young to compete on equal terms in what is fundamentally an unequal struggle and to equip them, as citizens of a democratic society, to be able to challenge whatever it is that is amiss in society at large. So much, briefly, for equal opportunities.

So far I have considered reducing the level of discrimination and providing equal opportunities. The third element in the Commission's work concerns improving relationships. Relationships are not improved in the abstract. One of the criticisms of multicultural education, as it has sometime been interpreted, is that merely swapping meals, socializing between majority and minority groups is not going to, in any deep way, improve relationships which are structually unsound in other ways. But of course there is a need for citizens of this country to know more about each other. Schools are about knowledge rather than ignorance. Even if that knowledge does not bring wisdom and affection for others, ignorance certainly can do the opposite. For example, the worries about immigration in this country are not just based on prejudice. They are based on ignorance. The country is filling up with people from overseas, some people believe. The truth is that about half a million more people have left the country in the last decade than have come in. Simple information of this kind reduces irrational fears.

There is a role for straightforward information: an attack on ignorance is the key thing that one is after.

Finally, again from the Commission's point of view, I want to pick on one example of what I would describe as a common-sense policy issue. The Inner London Education Authority recently published research on performance in junior schools. What that research is saying is that, so far as under-performance is concerned, there is a wide variation between the way in which individual schools are functioning. That difference remains when you have taken account of all the usual indicators, from family size to family background, parental income and degree of concern for education. That wide variation is explicable only by factors relating to the way the different schools are functioning. Things are or are not happening within school which significantly affect the output in terms of performance of the young people. The research showed that in a school where all children were doing well (for schools which did well tended to do well by all the children, the ablest and the least able) the black youngsters in those schools, the one who are supposed to be under-performing, were not under-performing at all. They were making the same degree of improvement as anybody else. But in the schools which were doing badly by everybody, the black youngsters also did poorly; but they were doing no worse than the other children in the school. Unfortunately, the black youngsters were found to be disproportionately located in the schools which were doing badly by everybody. In short, they were in the bad schools. To sum up, when they were in the good schools they were doing well and when they were in the less competent schools they were doing badly; and too many of them were in the bad schools.

The next question the research answered was 'Are the schools which are doing badly by all the children doing badly because so many black children are in them?' The researchers' answer is 'no', because some of the schools which were doing badly by all children had hardly any black children in them and some of the schools which were doing well by all children had lots of black children in them.

The lesson I draw from this research is that policy in educating all children for a multi-ethnic society need not be as complex as sometimes supposed. Straightforward well-run schools underpin what is needed. The things which make for good performance are no secret. That ILEA research places the responsibility back in the school where it ought to be; and we need to think hard about its implications. When all is said and done, the worst thing we could do would be to teach the children of ethnic minority citizens disproportionately badly. Education for all cannot be based on the systematic mis-education of some.

APPENDIX: Fact Sheet: Ethnic Minority Young People

Unemployment

1 *Ethnic minority young people have higher unemployment rates than their white counterparts*

On average, their unemployment rates are twice as high:

Labour Force Survey 1984 (DE Gazette, December 1985)

Males, aged 16–24	*Females, aged 16–24*
Whites — 20 per cent were unemployed	Whites — 15 per cent were unemployed
Asian origin — 25 per cent were unemployed	Asians — 35 per cent were unemployed
West Indian origin — 40 per cent were unemployed	West Indians — 25 per cent were unemployed

In many inner city areas, unemployment rates for ethnic minority young people are far higher:

Sheffield Careers Service Data, 1985
73 per cent of young black people were unemployed, compared with 47 per cent of young whites.

Bradford Careers Service Data 1984 (School Leavers)
7.5 per cent of 16-year old ethnic minority job seekers found work
32 per cent of whites found work
21.7 per cent of 18 year-old ethnic minority seekers found work
48.2 per cent of whites found work.

West Midlands County Council Data, 1984
White fifth form school leavers were three times as likely as Afro-Caribbeans to find jobs, and two-and-a-half times as likely as Asians.

Discrimination

2   *Ethnic minority young people face high levels of racial discrimination in selection for jobs*

> *Policy Studies Institute Survey 1984–5* — 'Racial Discrimination: 17 Years After the Act'

At least one third of the employers covered in the study discriminated against Asian applicants, or West Indian applicants, or both. Discrimination rates for those in the 18–20 age group were slightly higher.

CRE enquiries
Cases of 'pressure to discriminate', reported to the CRE by careers officers and others, indicate racial discrimination by employers, including those offering work placements to YTS trainees on mode B schemes. These have often been taken through the industrial tribunal process.

Examples:
'We can't take a black trainee — The customers wouldn't like it'
'We can't send a black trainee into people's home'
'Our staff wouldn't work with a black person'

Youth Training Scheme

3   *Ethnic minority young people are under-represented on employer led YTS courses*

Manchester, 1985
100 mode A schemes had no black trainees
44 per cent black trainees were concentrated in six out of 279 schemes.

Birmingham, 1984
Ten out of twenty-seven large company schemes had black trainees. Afro-Caribbean young people formed 8.9 per cent of all YTS trainees in the area, but only 2.8 per cent of those on large companies' unit schemes.

Peter Newsam

Bradford careers service statistics

December 1984			December 1985		
Mode	Ethnic Origin (%)		Mode	Ethnic Origin (%)	
	Black	White		Black	White
A	10.04	89.96	A	7.98	91.02
B1	28.03	71.97	B1	30.13	69.87
(= Training Workshop, CP & ITEC)			(= Training Workship, CP & ITEC)		
B2	67.14	32.86	B2	63.77	36.23
(= Community led)			(= Community led)		

The CRE Study — Racial Equality and the Youth Training Scheme (1984) and the *Bristol University Study* — Ethnic Minorities and the Youth Training Scheme (MSC, 1984) both confirmed under-representation of ethnic minority trainees on employers' schemes, particularly outside London and in the *private sector.*

4   *Ethnic minority young people are under-represented among those taken into employment after YTS*

   MSC Survey of YTS Leavers, April to August 1985
   68 per cent of white *mode A* leavers found jobs, compared with
   47 per cent of African/Caribbean leavers and
   44 per cent of Asian leavers.

   38 per cent of white *mode B1* leavers found jobs, compared with
   31 per cent of African/Caribbean leavers and
   26 per cent of Asian leavers.

   White leavers from all modes were more likely than ethnic minority leavers to find jobs with the same employer.

   Educational Qualifications

5   *Unemployment levels for ethnic minority people with qualifications are higher than those for white people in the same qualification bands*

   Labour Force Survey, 1981
   9 per cent of white men with '0' levels were unemployed compared with 25 per cent Afro-Caribbeans and 18 per cent of Asians. The rates for women showed similar differences. 1984 figures repeat this pattern.

6   *Ethnic minority young people are less likely to find employment after YTS than similarly qualified white leavers*

   MSC YTS Leavers survey, April-August 1985

Those with Grade 1 CSE, '0' or 'A' level qualifications
67 per cent of white YTS leavers were in a job, compared with
54 per cent of Asians and
37 per cent of Afro-Caribbeans.

39 per cent of whites were in a job with the same employer, compared with
37 per cent of Asians and
14 per cent of Afro-Caribbeans.

CSE and similar qualifications
55 per cent of white leavers were in a job (29 per cent with the same employer) compared with
19 per cent of Asians (9 per cent with same employer)
36 per cent of Afro-Caribbeans (21 per cent with same employer).

No Qualifications
33 per cent of white leavers were in a job (15 per cent with the same employer) compared with
30 per cent of Asians (11 per cent with same employer) and
14 per cent of Afro-Caribbeans (5 per cent with same employer).

Note: The Asian sample was very low; figures are therefore less reliable.

Further Reading

CRE Guidance Booklet — *Equal Opportunity and the Youth Training Scheme.*
CRE Guidance Booklet — *Positive Action and Equal Opportunity in Employment.*

Reference

COMMITTEE OF INQUIRY INTO THE EDUCATION OF CHILDREN FROM ETHNIC MINORITY GROUPS (1985) *Education for All.* (Swann Report) Cmnd. 9453, London, HMSO.

PART 2
OUTCOMES

7   West Indian and Asian Children's Educational Attainment

N.J. Mackintosh, C.G.N. Mascie-Taylor and A.M. West

Introduction

Public concern over the educational attainments of recently immi-grated children seems to have first become noticeable in the late 1960s, and from 1970 on a modest but steady stream of reports, analyses and discussions have been published. The focus of this concern, although at times concentrated exclusively on children of West Indian origin, has usually included two other main groups, children of Indian and of Pakistani origin. In earlier days, this already crude grouping, which quite clearly ignores a whole host of sub-groups within these three main groupings, was made cruder still by combining the latter two groups into a category of 'Asian'. In a survey of published data we can be no less crude than the reports we survey; we too therefore will usually have to resort to these very broad groupings.

The Earlier Picture

The earlier studies yielded a rather consistent picture. Recent immigrants, regardless of their origins, found the adjustment to British schools difficult, and obtained relatively low scores on formal tests of attainment, such as reading and mathematics, as well as on IQ tests. The longer the children had been in this country, the better they did, and in the case of Asian children, they often did as well as, or better than, the indigenous majority. But although the performance of West Indian children also improved with length of stay in Britain, even in the case of children born in this country, there remained a substantial gap between the West Indian minority and the indigenous majority. By 1985, the position was summarized in the Swann Report thus: 'West Indian children on average are underachieving at school ... Asian children, by contrast, show on average a pattern of achievement which resembles that of white children's (Swann, 1985, p. 89).

It is not necessary to present data from, or even to summarize, all the studies which pointed to these conclusions, for they have been reviewed elsewhere (Mackintosh and Mascie-Taylor, 1985; Taylor, 1981; Taylor and Hegarty, 1986). One set of data that will serve is that from the National Child Development Study of approximately 15,000 children born in a single week of 1958. In 1969, aged 11, they were given a variety of educational tests, IQ, reading and mathematics, and the results of these tests are shown in table 1, for three main groups, whites, West Indian and Asian, with the latter two groups sub-divided into those who had arrived in Britain within the last four years and those here longer than that. Longer residence in Britain improved the performance of both groups on all tests, but whereas it allowed the Asian children more or less to catch up with whites (except on reading), the West Indian children still lagged behind (Asian children actually born in Britain had a mean IQ identical to that of white children). The advantage of the NCDS data is that the children must be regarded as a representative cross-section of the entire population; the disadvantage is that the number of minority children (particularly long resident Asians) is relatively small; but other studies have confirmed that this group performed well on both educational and IQ tests (for example, Ashby, Morrison and Butcher, 1970; Little, 1975; Scarr *et al.*, 1983).

This last study, by Scarr *et al.*, differs from earlier ones, not only by being more recent, but also by showing that Indian and possibly Pakistani children (the numbers in this latter group are very small) although obtaining IQ scores hardly different from those of white children of 11 or 12, obtained rather low scores at age 8; unlike West Indian children, they showed substantial gains between these two ages. The data are shown in table 2. Scarr *et al.*, also reported data from GCE and CSE exams and from university entrance which suggested that the pattern of differences apparent by age 12 was maintained, West Indian children lagging far behind white and Indian children, who did not differ from one another. The most extensive data on this point were published by Swann (1985), and table 3 reproduces the results of a survey of school leavers from six (1978/79) and five (1981/82) LEAs. The new and surely welcome finding is that West

Table 1: National Child Development Study (1969) IQ, reading and mathematics scores for 11-year-old white, West Indian and Asian Children

		IQ	Reading	Mathematics
White	(n = 10,299)	100.6	100.6	100.9
West Indian	4 or more years in UK (N = 74)	89.0	90.0	88.2
	Less than 4 years in UK (N = 39)	82.3	83.0	82.3
Asian	4 or more years in UK (N = 25)	98.6	96.5	97.6
	Less than 4 years in UK (N = 37)	82.9	77.8	78.9

All scores have been standardized to a mean of 100, SD of 15 for the entire sample.

Table 2: IQ scores at ages 8, 11 and 12 for white, West Indian, Indian and Pakistani children

	8 years	11 years	12 years
White (N = 167)	106.7	107.8	105.2
West Indian (N = 112)	98.3	98.7	96.4
Indian (N = 90)	97.0	107.0	102.8
Pakistani (N = 16)	92.2	103.2	100.8

Source: Scarr *et al*, 1983, table 9.

Indian children are showing a small but significant improvement over this relatively short period of time, but otherwise the picture is a familiar one: the gap between West Indian and white children remains large; Asian children cannot be distinguished from whites.

Possible Changes in the Last Ten Years

Even the more recent data shown in table 3 are from children who left school in 1981/82 and must therefore have been born in the mid-1960s. They are of nearly the same generation as the children surveyed in NCDS and other studies published in the early 1970s. Some of the children from the Scarr *et al.* study were born somewhat later. Their data were collected in 1980/81 when the children ranged in age from 12 to 18. But a breakdown of the data shown in table 2 by the children's date of birth shows no obvious changes over time.

The picture presented by all these data, then, is one of initially poor performance by recent immigrants regardless of their ethnic origin, followed by reasonably steady improvement. In the case of

Table 3:   Percentage of white, West Indian and Asian children obtaining various GCE examination results and entering university

	5 or more higher grades at '0' level and CSE		1 or more 'A' level		Entering university	
	1978/79	1981/82	1978/79	1981/82	1978/79	1982/82
White*	16	19	12	13	3	4
West Indian	3	6	2	5	0	1
Asian	17	17	12	13	3	4

* The category in fact represents 'all other school leavers' of whom the majority were presumably white.
Source: Swann, 1985.

Table 4:   Child Health and Education Study (1980) IQ, reading and mathematics scores for 10-year-old white, West Indian, Indian and Pakistani children

	IQ	Reading	Mathematics
White (N = 10,812)	100.4	100.8	100.8
West Indian (N = 125)	92.3	90.3	88.1
Indian (N = 170)	91.9	93.1	93.0
Pakistani (N = 91)	89.3	88.6	89.5

Asian children, this catching up process seems to have been complete by the mid-1970s; in the case of West Indians, it clearly was not; but the data of table 3 suggest that their performance in school exams may still be slowly improving. The picture might encourage complacency. But we fear that the complacency may be misplaced; the picture may no longer be true.

The first suggestion of this comes from our analysis of the Child Health and Education Study, a study similar to NCDS of approximately 15,000 children born in a single week of 1970 and given a variety of educational tests at age 10 in 1980. The results are shown in table 4. Virtually all of these children were born in Britain and the exclusion of the small handful that were not does not alter the picture. By comparison with NCDS, West Indian children have slightly narrowed the IQ gap separating them from whites, but the two Asian groups have fallen back to the point where the Pakistani children obtain IQ scores lower than those of West Indian children. On the reading and maths tests, the Indian children do significantly better than the West Indians, although still not as well as whites, while the Pakistani children outscore West Indians on mathematics but fall below them on reading.

It would be a mistake to make too much of this comparison between NCDS and CHES. The actual tests employed in the two

Table 5:   Scores on various tests for 7, 9, and 11-year-old-children in three south-east Midlands towns (1985/86)

	Vocabulary	Non-verbal Reasoning	Reading	Mathematics
White (N = 531–537)	100	100	100	100
Pakistani (N = 439–448)	85.9	85.8	84.5	91.6
Indian (N = 254–259)	89.6	89.6	90.7	96.0
West Indian (N = 51–52)	95.6	91.8	97.2	93.4

All scores are standardized to a mean of 100, SD of 15, for the white sample, at each age separately.

studies were quite different, and were given to the children at slightly different ages (recall that Scarr *et al.* reported that Indian children performed no better than West Indians at age 8 but had caught up with whites by age 12). Nevertheless, just as our confidence in the reliability of the NCDS data is justified by their agreement with most other studies of about that time, so it should be possible to test the reliability of the CHES data by comparing them with other contemporary studies. Unfortunately, there are none. The nearest to a contemporary study is that of Scarr *et al.*, where the children were born between 1962 and 1968, i.e., all older than those of CHES. Nevertheless, since there is no suggestion from their data of a decline in the Indian children's scores over time, there is a suggestion of some disagreement.

In a preliminary attempt to resolve this conflict we have, with the cooperation of the LEAs concerned, started collecting data from children of various ethnic minorities, so far from schools in three towns, with children 7, 9, and 11 years old. All children were given vocabulary and non-verbal reasoning tests, as well as tests of reading and mathematics; and the results of these tests are shown in table 5. The largest minority group in those schools is children of Pakistani origin, and it is clear that their scores lag well behind those of white children on all tests. The gap is no smaller in non-verbal reasoning and mathematics than in vocabulary and reading. Bearing in mind the sample sizes concerned, it is also worth noting that Pakistani children obtain considerably lower scores than West Indian children, while, except on mathematics, the Indian children also performed slightly worse than the West Indians.

Our study, unlike that of Scarr *et al.* (1983) is so far exclusively cross-sectional rather than longitudinal. Moreover, we also, so far, have far too few West Indian children to look at their breakdown by age. But there are enough white, Indian and Pakistani children to do this, and the answer is that there is no suggestion that the gap between them narrows between the ages of 7 and 11.

In so far as these results differ from those reported by Scarr *et al.*, the differences could be due to a number of factors. They might represent secular changes from the mid- to late-1970s to the mid-1980s. Or they might reflect differences in the populations sampled. Neither their data nor ours can safely be generalized to the country as a whole: the population of a single town is not representative of the population of the entire country.

But it would be foolish to exaggerate the differences. The major discrepancy is in the scores for Pakistani children. But Scarr *et al.*'s data suggest the possibility of some difference between Indian and Pakistani children, and given the size of their Pakistani sample, the discrepancy may be merely a matter of chance. Taken together with the CHES data, these new results suggest to us that confident claims about 'Asian' children's educational attainments may no longer be entirely justified. While West Indian children may indeed be continuing to catch up with whites, some Asian children may not be doing as well as those born ten or twenty years earlier.

Accounts of Ethnic Differences in Educational Attainment

We have no intention of attempting to provide a comprehensive explanation of the entire pattern of differences in educational attainment that we have briefly reviewed. It is, after all, most improbable that any single factor will ever be found sufficient at all times and in all places to account for the performance of all ethnic minorities (cf. Verma, 1985). Children whose first language is not English and who speak some other language at home are unlikely to read English as well as their English-speaking contemporaries. But this factor, obviously applicable to some groups, is largely irrelevant to others. Similarly, the relatively poor performance of recently arrived immigrants is both unsurprising and unlikely to be always explained by the same factors as are responsible for the continued poor performance of children born in this country.

But it would be little short of disingenuous to stop short at this point, and we believe it worth commenting briefly on a few possibilities. The first is that the differences we have surveyed are not real, but artefactual consequences of the use of patently inappropriate and biased tests. This is a charge commonly brought against the use of IQ tests with ethnic minorities. We do not wish to make large claims on behalf of IQ tests. We are inclined to believe that a child's IQ score is important only in so far as it predicts other things about him — how well he is doing at school, whether he is likely to pass various exams, gain entrance to university and so on. It is, of course, just here that the argument is directed, it being widely believed that IQ scores do not predict educational attainment in minority groups. But the belief is almost totally unfounded. A cursory examination of tables 1 and 4 will confirm that there is a reasonably close relationship between a particular group's performance on IQ tests and their educational attainment as measured by reading and mathematics tests. And *within* each ethnic group in these tables, the correlations between IQ scores and reading and mathematics scores are uniformly high, of the order of .70 (Mackintosh and Mascie-Taylor, 1985; see also Scarr *et al.*, 1983). What is not always so apparent from tables 1 and 4 is that where there are discrepancies between an ethnic minority's IQ scores and their educational attainment, it is more often than not the case that their IQ scores overestimate their scores on tests of reading and mathematics (Mackintosh and Mascie-Taylor, 1985). Regression analyses establish that they often obtain *lower* scores on reading and mathematics tests than do white children of comparable IQ. As is shown in figure 1, this is particularly true of West Indian children in CHES and, less surprisingly, of some of the groups of Asian children on tests of reading. A similar effect is shown in Dawson's contribution to this volume. In her study, Afro-Caribbean children obtained lower scores than European children on tests of reading and mathematics, and continued to do so even when allowance was made for their inferior performance on a test of non-verbal reasoning ('IQ'). In other words, they obtained worse scores on reading and mathematics than their 'IQ' score would predict. The same was true for Asian children's performance on the reading test.

It is worth mentioning one implication of this. A second common belief is that the reason why children from ethnic minorities fail at school is because they are discriminated against: in one version of this argument, teachers are said to hold stereotyped opinions about their abilities and the children live down to these low expectations. The problem with this explanation, as we have argued elsewhere (Mackintosh and Mascie-Taylor, 1985) is that there is no good evid-

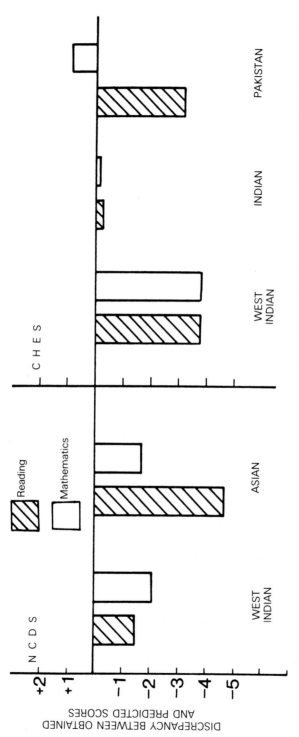

Difference between obtained and predicted scores on reading and mathematics test for ethnic minority children in NCDS and CHES. Predicted scores are those predicted on the basis of the children's IQ scores if the relationship between IQ and reading and mathematics scores were exactly the same in minority groups as it was in white children.

ence that a child's IQ score is affected by his teacher's expectations in this way. And to the extent that the scholastic achievement of children from minority groups simply reflects their IQ scores, it is unlikely that their poor achievement can be blamed solely on their teachers' low expectations of them. But note that their school achievement often lags behind their IQ scores. Since there is excellent evidence that how well a child learns at school can be affected by his teacher's expectations of him, it is possible that one reason why children from minority groups do not always do as well at school as their IQ scores would lead one to expect, is precisely because of their teachers' low expectations?

A third possibility, to which we alluded briefly above, is that the data we have surveyed are far too crude, not just because paper and pencil tests provide an imperfect measure of scholastic attainment, but because all studies lump together quite disparate groups of children. The West Indies are a group of by no means homogeneous islands, and what may be true of children whose families originated from one island and arrived in Britain in the 1950s, may be quite untrue of children from other islands who emigrated at a later date. And this diversity pales into insignificance by comparison with that evident among 'Asian' children. Even the crude distinction between Indian and Pakistani children is sufficient to suggest some differences in performance. But it is possible that this overall difference conceals a much more complex pattern of similarities and differences between various subgroups. One possibility, alluded to by Swann (1985), is that children of Bangladeshi origin obtain particularly low scores, and their inclusion among Pakistanis is responsible for the low average performance of the Pakistani group. Our own data provide no support for this speculation. The ninety-one children from Pakistan in CHES include, it is true, seven children from Bangladesh, but their mean IQ, at 91.8, is marginally higher than that of the remaining Pakistani children (89.2). The data shown in table 5 include no children from Bangladesh at all: such Bangladeshi children as we have found in these schools obtain scores on all tests no different from those of the larger Pakistani group.

It may well be, as Swann believed, that Bangladeshi children are experiencing particular difficulty in adjusting to British schools, but it would probably be wrong to single them out as a unique 'problem' group. What may sometimes be a significant contributory factor to the poor average performance of Pakistani children is that Pakistani girls obtain particularly low scores. In CHES, the difference between Pakistani boys and girls was 4.5 points in IQ, 4.3 points on maths and even 2.2 points on reading (where in all other ethnic groups, girls did better than boys). Pakistani boys, with an IQ of 91.3 did not differ from West Indians or Indians. But even this may not always be important, for there is no similar sex difference in the data shown in table 5.

There is yet another way in which we may be misled by large-scale social surveys. The very large majority of children in recent studies are classified as having been born in Britain; this suggests that they should no longer be subject to the problems and difficulties experienced by new immigrants. But as was noted by the Swann Report in the case of Bangladeshi children (Swann, 1985, pp 124–5), and as we have discovered when testing in schools, teachers commented with some despair on the practice common to some Pakistani families of removing their children from school for extended visits home, often lasting up to a year or more. The fact that these children were born in Britain does not imply that they have been continuously educated in this country and it does not seem particularly surprising that their educational achievement should suffer.

There is one final possibility that we believe merits serious consideration, namely that educational attainment is related to social circumstances and the social circumstances of some groups of immigrant children have changed over the past ten years or so. It will come as no surprise to anyone to learn that the social circumstances of most ethnic minorities differ markedly from those of the white majority. Both in NCDS and in CHES, for example, West Indian children differ in many ways from whites, with a higher percentage having fathers in manual occupations, living in a household with no male head or with four or more children and overcrowded, with a lower family income and so on. All of these factors are related to IQ scores among indigenous children and it seems possible that they might also contribute to the average differences in IQ scores between groups. When West Indian children are compared to white children matched in terms of these social circumstances, the difference in their IQ scores are substantially reduced, to 5.2 points in NCDS and to 2.6 in CHES (Mackintosh and Mascie-Taylor, 1985). But changes in social circumstances over time may also contribute to the differences between NCDS and CHES. In 1969 the Asian children in NCDS who had been in Britain for four or more years, were not suffering the same degree of social deprivation as West Indian children. But by 1980, there had been a decline in their fortunes, and in terms of the social variables we analyzed in CHES, Pakistani children were living

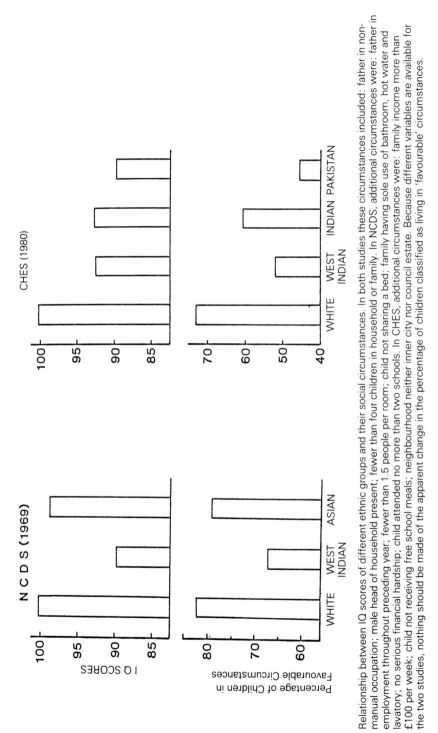

Relationship between IQ scores of different ethnic groups and their social circumstances. In both studies these circumstances included: father in non-manual occupation; male head of household present; fewer than four children in household or family. In NCDS, additional circumstances were: father in employment throughout preceding year; fewer than 1.5 people per room; child not sharing a bed; family having sole use of bathroom, hot water and lavatory; no serious financial hardship; child attended no more than two schools. In CHES, additional circumstances were: family income more than £100 per week; child not receiving free school meals; neighbourhood neither inner city nor council estate. Because different variables are available for the two studies, nothing should be made of the apparent change in the percentage of children classified as living in 'favourable' circumstances.

in even less favourable circumstances than West Indian children. Figure 2 provides a graphic representation of the correlation between IQ scores and social circumstances that holds across the two studies. The correlation is far from perfect, and correlation, as we know, does not entail causal connection. But correlation is certainly consistent with causation and the data shown in this figure do suggest the possibility that the changing pattern of educational attainment of minority groups may be connected with changes in their social circumstances.

Conclusions

The generally received opinion is that the 'problem' of the educational attainment of children from ethnic minorities amounts to this: newly arrived immigrants tend to find it very difficult to adjust to British schools, but the longer they have lived in this country, the better they cope; 'Asian' children, indeed, soon come to perform at a level indistinguishable from the white majority. But children of West Indian origins continue to lag behind the indigenous majority. There is reason to believe that this picture may no longer be entirely accurate. Children of Pakistani origin, it appears, are now obtaining rather lower scores on standard tests of attainment and of IQ than are West Indian children. There is some disagreement between different studies whether Indian children are continuing to perform at the same level as whites or whether they have slipped back.

We have briefly considered some factors that may contribute to this changing pattern of differences in attainment. This may lay us open to the change of showing 'an obsessive concern with "explaining" this [underachievement] rather than focusing on factors which might make for children's improved education' (Tomlinson, 1983, p. 4). But although it is obvious that our discussion is necessarily speculative, it seems odd to suppose that explanation and looking for improvement are necessarily antagonistic exercises.

References

ASHBY, B. MORRISON, A. and BUTCHER, H.J. (1970) 'The abilities and attainments of immigrant children, *Research in Education*, 4, pp 73–80.
LITTLE, A. (1975) 'Performance of children from ethnic minority backgrounds in primary schools', *Oxford Review of Education*, 1, 2, pp 117–35.
MACKINTOSH, N.J. and MASCIE-TAYLOR, C.G.N. (1985) 'The IQ question',

in COMMITTEE OF INQUIRY INTO THE EDUCATION OF CHILDREN FROM ETHNIC MINORITY GROUPS *Education for All* (Swann Report) Cmnd 9453, London, HMSO, pp 126–63.

SCARR, S., CARPARULO, B.K., FERDMAN, B.M., TOWER, R.B. and CAPLAN, J. (1983) 'Developmental status and school achievements of minority and non-minority children from birth to 18 years in a British Midlands town', *British Journal of Developmental Psychology*, 1, 1, pp 31–8.

SWANN, M. (1985) *Education for All: A Brief Guide to the Main Issues of the Report*, London, HMSO.

TAYLOR, M. (1981) *Caught Between, A Review of Research into the Education of Pupils of West Indian Origin*, Windsor, NFER. Educational Research.

TAYLOR, M. and HEGARTY, S. (1986) *Between Two Cultures*. Windsor, NFER.

TOMLINSON, S. (1983) *Ethnic Minorities in British Schools*, London, Heinemann.

VERMA, G.K. (1985) 'Summary of the main findings of a longitudinal study', in THE COMMITTEE OF INQUIRY INTO THE EDUCATION OF CHILDREN FROM ETHNIC MINORITY GROUPS *Education for All* (Swann Report), Cmnd 9453, London, HMSO, pp 167–70.

8   Educational Achievement of Ethnic Minority Children in a Midlands Town

John R. Roberts

Summary

Results are reported from an investigation by Scarr *et al* (1983) into the comparative development and educational achievement of children from ethnic minorities in a Midlands town. Differences are shown in pre-school language and stimulation, primary school literacy, and verbal and non-verbal reasoning skills, secondary school placement and examination success, and post-school outcomes. On the average British children of parents of West Indian origins do least well, whilst British children of parents of Indian origins move through delays to sometimes overtake their majority peers. Subsequent developments in local policy and provision are outlined. The importance of evaluating interventions is underlined.

In the following chapter British children of parents of West Indian origins are designated BWI and British children of parents of Indian origins are designated BI.

Introduction

In the Midlands town where I work, unanimous, informed local opinion has expressed concern over some years that children from certain ethnic minority groups achieve less well at school compared with their peers from the majority community. These views were supported by clear, general evidence in the literature, for example, Yule *et al.* (1975), and more recently the ILEA Literacy Survey (1980) and the Interim Report of the Swann Committee (Committee of Inquiry into the Education of Children from Ethnic Minority Groups, 1981). Other contributions in the 'Outcomes' section of this book provide more recent details (Chapters 7 and 9–12).

The present author, working with the local Community Relations Council, planned a self-help scheme for the West Indian community. This scheme failed to obtain funding from the Home Office in 1978 and again in 1979 when it was described as 'too small'. Despite this rejection, it was considered that the issue was far too important to be dropped. Thinking bigger eventually led the Community Relations Officer to Professor Sandra Scarr at Yale University. She subsequently visited England, had full discussions, then raised an American team, planned the project and returned to gather data in November 1980. The present author had no responsibility for the design, interpretation or writing up of that project. His role was that of sounding board, facilitator and subsequently one enactor of recommendations to the LEA.

This chapter will first report a selection of Scarr's findings, focussing on factors associated with successful education as it is widely perceived. Data for Pakistani children are omitted, since their number were small in this particular study.

Pre-School Children (0–5 Years)

Every town health visitor was interviewed and a total survey of health records conducted to identify all ethnic minority pre-schoolers. A comparison group from the majority comunity was formed. Standard informations about all these children were obtained.

Tables 1 and 2 indicate that in the opinion of health visitors the minority households were less well equipped with play materials and were less good at offering developmentally appropriate stimulation. The households in which BWI pupils lived were relatively the most disadvantaged.

Table 1: *Percentages of health visitor ratings of pre-school child's physical environment*

	West Indian	Indian	Majority
Households with inadequate play materials	32% (22/68)*	16% (19/121)	6% (9/149)

(* Numbers in brackets indicate numbers of children e.g. 22 out of a total of 68 children.)

Table 2: *Means of health visitor ratings of family interaction for pre-school child on 3-point scale (1 = low, 2 = medium, 3 = high)*

	West Indian	Indian	Majority
Developmentally appropriate stimulation	2.01 (68)	2.10 (119)	2.52 (149)

John R. Roberts

Table 3: *Percentages of items passed by pre-school child on the Sheridan Developmental Screening Test for hearing/speech and language development*

Age at testing	West Indian %	Indian %	Majority %
0–6 months	95.4 (31)	98.2 (63)	95.1 (92)
7–12 months	93.1 (42)	95.5 (84)	95.2 (99)
13–21 months	82.6 (14)	94.1 (31)	92.1 (33)
22–30 months	80.8 (25)	93.0 (38)	95.3 (57)
31–48 months	83.4 (7)	86.3 (21)	86.3 (14)

N.B. In this table only the bracketed figures are the number of observations available at each level, not the number of children in each age group.

Table 4: *Mean quotients of intelligence test scores from three group tests in the primary school*

	West Indian	Indian	Majority
Young Non-Readers I.Q. (age 8)	98.1 (230)	97.9 (235)	106.1 (364)
Moray House 12+ Verbal Reasoning I.Q. (average of two tests)	93.6 (253)	98.7 (216)	103.3 (361)
NFER Non-Verbal D-H I.Q. (age 12)	97.2 (205)	103.9 (173)	106.8 (338)

Table 3 suggests that BWI youngsters developed more slowly in the areas of hearing, speech and language, as sampled by the Sheridan tests administered by doctors and health visitors. Proportionally more BWI children were referred to the Child Development Centre because of delays in language development (British–West Indian 10.5 per cent; British–Indian 4.1 per cent; Majority 2.7 per cent).

Primary School Children (5–12 Years)

Headteachers were interviewed and a total survey of school records was made to identify all minority children. A comparison majority sample was formed by randomly selecting school record cards of children of the same age and sex attending the same school. Standard informations were extracted from the record cards for all these children.

Table 4 indicated that majority children on the average functioned consistently better than their minority peers in the reasoning skills sampled. BWI children showed no measurable gains from the age of 8 to 12, whereas BI youngsters significantly raised their cognitive performance, especially on the non-verbal tests.

Table 5 shows no disparity in reading between the ethnic groups

Table 5: *Mean reading ages in years for primary schoolchildren*

Age Group		West Indian	Indian	Majority
First School	(5:00	6.2 (31)	6.5 (25)	6.2 (35)
	(6:00	6.7 (99)	7.1 (95)	6.9 (112)
	(7:00	7.7 (187)	7.8 (205)	8.0 (273)
	(8:00	8.5 (228)	8.7 (231)	8.8 (327)
Middle School	(9:00	9.1 (230)	9.3 (213)	9.7 (338)
	(10:00	9.8 (204)	10.0 (173)	10.7 (305)
	(11:00	10.7 (181)	10.8 (133)	11.5 (293)
	(12:00	11.5 (136)	11.4 (98)	12.2 (177)

Table 6: *Percentages of secondary school pupils placed in grammar schools/streams, including sixth formers*

West Indian	Indian	Majority
2.5%	17.5%	30.1%
(7/281)	(50/285)	(1727/5735)

Table 7: *Setting of secondary school pupils for English and mathematics in percentages*

	West Indian	Indian	Majority
Remedial English	17%	12%	5%
	(30/176)	(23/188)	(13/239)
Remedial maths	19%	12%	8%
	(42/216)	(26/224)	(25/304)
Top stream English	20%	36%	34%
	(35/176)	(67/188)	(81/239)
Top stream maths	19%	37%	33%
	(40/216)	(83/224)	(99/304)

during the First school years up to the age of 8, despite probable differences in language and experience. From the age of 9 the majority children pulled away consistently from their minority peers.

Secondary School Students (13–16 (–18) Years)

Headteachers were interviewed and again a total survey of school records made to identify all minority students. A comparison majority sample was randomly formed.

Table 6 demonstrates that BWI pupils rarely went to grammar schools. The BI students fared decidedly better, but still did poorly in relation to their majority peers.

The level or school set in which youngsters were initially placed is shown in table 7 and confirms the poorer academic standing of the

Table 8: *Percentages of secondary school pupils sitting GCE 'O' level examinations*

	West Indian	Indian	Majority
Any subject	9%	42%	42%
	(10/88)	(48/114)	(67/158)
English Language	1%	23%	34%
	(1/88)	(26/114)	(53/158)
Mathematics	7%	37%	27%
	(6/88)	(42/114)	(45/158)

Table 9: *Percentages of secondary school pupils passing GCE 'O' level and passing well*

	West Indian	Indian	Majority
English Language			
grades A, B, C,	8%	32%	35%
and CSE grade 1	(7/88)	(36/114)	(56/158)
Mathematics	16%	49%	37%
grades A, B, C,	(14/88)	(56/114)	(59/158)
and CSE grade 1			
English Language	1%	6%	19%
grades A and B	(1/88)	(7/114)	(30/158)
Mathematics	2%	25%	20%
grade A and B	(2/88)	(28/114)	(32/158)

BWI pupils. The BI students, perhaps with less developed reading skills, gained slightly more top stream places relative to the majority students. They were nonetheless over-represented in the two remedial streams.

Nearly all secondary pupils sat GCE or CSE examinations. Tables 8 and 9 indicate the differing percentages sitting and passing the more esteemed GCE in the two most highly regarded and occupationally valued subjects of English Language and mathematics. The BWI pupils as a group did poorly, whilst the BI pupils (who left their middle schools with reading achievements parallel to the BWI pupils) competed strongly with their majority peers, indeed surpassing them in mathematics.

Post-School Outcomes

Two hundred and fifty-one young men and women were traced who had left school over the previous two years. Table 10 shows some differences between the ethnic groups.

BI students used the college of further education to a considerable extent. Their BWI fellow students proved to be predominantly

Table 10: Disposition of young adults who had left secondary school over the previous two years in percentages

	West Indian	Indian	Majority
College of Further Education	41% (29/70) (21 women)	61% (57/93)	14% (12/84)
Higher education	4% (3/70) (All women)	14% (13/93)	8% (7/84)
Unemployed	20% (14/70) (13 men)	5% (5/93)	29% (24/84)
Unskilled employment	20% (14/70) (12 men)	2% (2/93)	26% (22/84)

female, comprising 75 per cent of the BWI women leavers traced. Majority leavers were very unrepresented at the college.

Echoing the same trend, more BI and BWI women (11 per cent of the women traced) proceeded to higher education.

Majority leavers went more frequently into unemployment or unskilled employment, as did the BWI men (19 per cent and 17 per cent respectively).

Summary of the Research Results

These findings from birth to young adulthood illustrate how children from minority ethnic backgrounds lagged behind their majority peers, the discrepancy being more pronounced for the BWI pupils.

BWI children showed pre-school language delays, and subsequently at the primary school level lacked reading skills, and verbal and non-verbal reasoning skills. They were placed less advantageously in their secondary schools and succeeded less well with examinations. On leaving school, the BWI men showed little interest in continuing their education, took poor jobs or were unemployed. The BWI women by contrast seemed eager to grasp new educational opportunities. The Scarr study did not address possible causes of ethnic group differences in school achievements. It charted a cumulative deficit in the achievements of BWI pupils.

BI children exhibited the same lack of literacy and reasoning skills in the primary school, but were rather less disadvantageously placed in secondary schools, where they redressed their educational shortcomings and acquired examination results equal to and better than their majority peers. The BI pupils consolidated these gains by seizing further educational opportunities — very few became unemployed or took poor jobs.

The above findings describe the situation in the particular area. The results present a challenge to all members of all groups in the community.

Developments Following from the Concern Highlighted by the Research

New initiatives positively needed to be developed locally. Much consultation and thought went into the evolution of fresh policies and provisions. A number of initiatives instigated to address the problems identified are described and commented on below.

1   *Language and early stimulation* seem fundamentally relevant to the educational process. Ways of increasing parenting/caring skills here had to be pursued. Three specific developments have crystallized;

   (i)   Firstly, a Parents' Centre, known as the *Northlands Project*, was opened in September 1982 in premises on a First school site. It is run by a full-time teacher to provide guidance to parents, using discussion, demonstration and training, with individuals and groups at the Centre, in the homes of parents and elsewhere. Provision includes a toy library. Full liaison with other schools, nurseries, playgroups and all the relevant services, including adult education, has been essential. Similar projects have been run in other cities and towns in England (Widlake and Macleod, 1984).
   A second teacher was appointed in 1983 and this post is filled on an annual basis by teachers seconded from their schools, an arrangement which ensures the dissemination of the work of this highly successful Centre. A Manpower Services Commission helper works at the Centre and voluntary help is always sought. The Centre is open to parents of all children, since many majority families clearly need to profit from the same style of help.

   (ii)   Secondly, the Social Services Department advertised the job of *Pre-school Playgroup Adviser* for a social worker with special interests in ethnic minority groups. The appointment was made in June 1981: the quality and quantity of specialist advice to playgroups with minority children has thus increased.

A second appointment was made shortly after this of a *Gujerati-speaking Social Worker* who is undertaking research with the Asian community into the needs of younger children and the mental health of women.

(iii) Thirdly, a successful bid was made for a Government Education Support Grant for a Portage Project. *The Home Education Team* was established in September 1986 to provide home-based teaching programmes for pre-school children who show a delay in their development due to disadvantage or disability.

2 First schools seem to be teaching their children the basic *reading skills* successfully. This success needs to extend into middle schools so that development is heightened for all pupils in reading for comprehension, information and pleasure, and in the active skills of communication and writing. Debate continues about maintaining a formal, structured teaching of reading up to the age of 12, since it is recognized that this extension would necessarily displace other activities from the curriculum. There is no consensus as yet about its desirability.

3 Much consideration has been given to the possibility of teaching *thinking/reasoning skills* to make certain that equal opportunities exist for all ethnic groups to acquire such skills. The LEA retains a 12+ selection procedure and anything which resembles 'coaching' for this would be highly undesirable. The LEA suggested that initiatives in this area should come from independent organizations in the community. Discussions about teaching thinking skills have been held, but have not presently led to any illuminating sources nor identified any good practices. This is not to say that such cannot be found (for example, Feuerstein *et al.*, 1980). Knowledge about *study skills* is more advanced (Wolfenden and Pumfrey, 1985 and 1986) and is disseminating widely in secondary schools, but to a much lesser extent in middle schools. In-service training may be the way forward.

4 A programme to inform and counsel parents about ways of educationally motivating and assisting their children, encouraging them to value educational goals and to work for examinations, appears essential for Secondary pupils. No efficient strategies, however,

John R. Roberts

have materialized, whilst the need has become greater. The worsened employment prospects for school leavers is increasingly reported as debilitating pupil motivation to strive for examination success, particularly amongst the lower achievers. This must affect minority pupils disproportionately, since they are over-represented in the lower achievers and surveys confirm their job prospects to be worse because of racial prejudice.

The provision of a quiet, purposeful, out-of-school working situation was regarded as one desirable and achievable resource for those pupils whose homes were physically difficult or too distracting for study. In September 1984 the LEA established a *Homework Centre* at the College of Further Education, where direct, individual assistance and guidance could be offered to self-selecting students by an appointed and by additional volunteer teachers in an appropriate educational environment. At this same Centre advice would readily be available to parents. Local headteachers totally supported this scheme, as did the leaders of the ethnic minority communities.

The number of pupils attending, however, proved disappointing (averaging five with peaks of ten-twelve and troughs of one-two). Nor were the attenders ethnic minority pupils. A further considerable promotion of the Centre to headteachers, minority leaders and other significant community figures was conducted, along with newspaper advertisements. The venue was changed for three of the five evenings a week to a school sited centrally amidst the homes of the main population of minority families.

There was no improvement in usage and the project was reluctantly terminated after three terms. The organizer felt that pupils needed much more direct and sustained encouragement to attend than had been achieved. Perhaps the negative socio-economic climate also had its influence.

The Community Relations Council planned an *Educational Shop* which was run by volunteer teachers and others at a large store in the town centre on a Saturday. Professional advice and direction was given to enquiring parents. It is intended to repeat this event from time to time.

5 Unemployed school leavers may need help to develop certain skills, so as to maximize job prospects, and to re-establish feelings of personal adequacy and worth. A full-time teacher was appointed and a special *programme of classes* arranged by the College of Further Education in association with the Community Relations

Council. The classes were aimed at ethnic minority young people of 17 + years who need tuition in literacy and numeracy to help them benefit from subsequent courses. Counselling, advice and pastoral care were also included in the programme to offset negative self-attitudes.

After one year's experience the remit of these successful classes was broadened and they are currently operating as an *Education Workshop*.

6 Low expectation, intentional and unintentional racism, and stereotyping by teachers are all known to contribute to poor achievement and unhappiness, which consequently diminish life opportunities for pupils from ethnic minorities. Professor Scarr was not asked to research *teacher attitudes* in her project, so local knowledge about this highly significant area remains uncertain.

Extensive discussion about the Scarr findings were held amongst teachers, officers and advisory staff. These meetings provided a first stage in combatting any unhelpful attitudes which may exist in the education service.

Following these preliminaries, a variety of courses, talks, events and exhibitions around multi-ethnic themes have been and are continuing to be produced by the LEA. The following list illustrates the range:

(a) *Courses*
'Beyond Rampton — whither education in a multicultural society' [10 sessions] January–March 1982
'Attitudes and prejudices' [6 sessions] November–December 1983
'Education in and for a multicultural society' [1 session] May 1984
'Community relations and patterns of post war immigration locally' [2 sessions] October 1984
'Language in the multicultural classroom' [6 sessions] October–December 1984
Course for Section 11 teachers [4 sessions] June 1986

(b) *Events*
Visit to Sikh Temple — March 1983
Visit to Mosque — September 1983
Carribean week for Middle school children — October 1983
Carribean week for First school children — June 1984

(c) *Exhibitions*

African and Asian Resource Centre Exhibition — October 1985

Exhibition of multicultural materials — March 1986

The above activities can all be criticized on various grounds. Accepting this, they represent a growing awareness of the need to value the cultural diversity in the area.

7 The last and really major initiative taken by the LEA was in appointing an *Adviser for Multicultural Education* in April 1985. The energetic person appointed has developed an Intercultural Curriculum Support Service. From January 1987, this service will comprise some twenty full-time people:

5 advisory teachers for multicultural/non-racist education
7 team members work with them
3 home/school liaison teachers
2 coordinators for multicultural education
 (1 for primary schools and 1 for secondary schools)
3 bilingual peripatetic teachers

Half these posts are redesignations of existing ones and half are new, their funding coming under Section 11 of the Education Support Grant.

It can be optimistically anticipated that this well-resourced County service can spearhead, accelerate and consolidate developments to combat the circumstances which generate educational disadvantage for ethnic minority children.

One complex issue that will have to be addressed is the effects of the innovations initiated (Pumfrey, 1984). Such evaluation is controversial but essential.

Conclusion

Local anxieties about ethnic minority children have been factually confirmed by an authoritative study. The thoughtful analysis of the Scarr report has jolted any complacency, provoked new thinking and provided fresh impetus and resolve to tackle an important problem with priority. The findings and the responses of the LEA should stimulate some reappraisal in other authorities. As with many LEAs, concern was recognized and action implemented long before the Swann Report was published. The evaluation of the initiatives advocated to address the problem of minority ethnic group underachievement in educational is essential if effective practices are to be identified.

References

COMMITTEE OF INQUIRY INTO THE EDUCATION OF CHILDREN FROM ETHNIC MINORITY GROUPS (1982) *West Indian Children in Our Schools* (Rampton Report) Cmnd 8273, London, HMSO.

FEUERSTEIN, R. in collaboration with RAND, Y., HOFFMAN, M.B. and MILLER, R. (1980) *Instrumental Enrichment: An Intervention Programme for Cognitive Modifiability.* Baltimore, MD, University Park Press.

INNER LONDON EDUCATION AUTHORITY (1980) *Literacy Survey*, London, ILEA Research and Statistics Group.

PUMFREY, P.D. (Ed) (1984) 'Psychologists and minority ethnic groups', *Educational and Child Psychology*, 1, 1, pp 2–66.

SCARR, S., CAPARULO, B., FERDMAN, B., TOWERS, B. and CAPLAN, J. (1983) 'Developmental status and school achievements of minority and non-minority children from birth to 18 years in a British Midlands town, *British Journal of Developmental Psychology*, 1,1, pp 31–48.

WIDLAKE, P. and MACLEOD, F. (1984) *Raising Standards: Parental Involvement Programmes and the Language Performance of Children,* Coventry, Community Education Development Centre.

WOLFENDEN, M. and PUMFREY, P.D. (1985) 'A review of research: Students' study behaviour (part A)', *Educational Psychology in Practice*, 1,3, pp 91–9.

WOLFENDEN, M. and PUMFREY, P.D. (1986) 'A review of research: Students' study behaviour (part B)', *Educational Psychology in Practice*, 1, 4, pp 135–41.

YULE, W., BERGER, M., RUTTER, M. and YULE, B. (1975) 'Children of West Indian immigrants — Intellectual performance and reading attainment', *Journal of Child Psychology and Psychiatry*, 16, 1, pp 1–15.

9   Black Pupils' Progress in Secondary School

Barbara Maughan and Graham Dunn

In this chapter we focus on one particular minority group — black children of West Indian origin — and one particular aspect of their attainments: their progress, relative to whites, over the secondary school years. Questions of progress have been central, implicitly if not explicitly, to much of the debate in this field, and yet data that bear directly on them are still relatively limited. The great majority of studies to date have been cross-sectional in design, each individually exploring results for different samples at different age-groups. Piecing together this cross-sectional evidence from what might be described as the first generation of British research in the field, we know that black children of West Indian origin scored less well than whites on a range of tests of attainment early in the primary school years, and continued to do so right up to the end of secondary schooling (see Tomlinson, 1983). It is widely accepted that a complex interplay of factors is likely to underlie these differences. What is less clear, however, from this patchwork of studies, is whether the gap between the groups had narrowed appreciably between 7 and 16, or widened, or remained essentially the same. To answer this question, which is of major educational and developmental significance, we need directly longitudinal evidence, tracing the same groups of pupils as they progress through the school system.

Such direct evidence as is available at present is not only limited, but also somewhat inconsistent. Results from the National Child Development Study (Mackintosh and Mascie-Taylor, 1985) showed essentially similar rates of progress in black and white children's reading between the ages of 11 and 16. Other studies have reached less optimistic conclusions. Perhaps the most widely known are results from the Inner London Education Authority's Literacy Survey, which charted the reading attainments of one whole age-group of London children from eight to 15 (Mabey, 1981). Despite considerable losses from the original sample over the course of the study, the numbers of black children represented were still substantial (n = 1465). Over the seven-year period of the research, black pupils' scores declined by comparison with whites' by some four standardized points. There are indications in the report that much of this decline may have occurred among black children born and fully educated in the UK. The main concern, then, that forms the background to our study, is the possibility that black pupils fall further behind during their schooling, perhaps in response to low teacher expectations or other negative school experiences.

Our own study provides further data on these questions, from a smaller but similarly London-based sample from the 1970s. Despite the fact that longitudinal data give us the best basis for assessing relative progress over time, there are nevertheless a number of difficulties inherent in analyzing data of this kind. After presenting a brief overview of some of our findings (reported more fully in Maughan *et al.*, 1985; and Maughan and Rutter, 1986), we conclude with some more general comments on the problems to be faced in any progress studies of this kind.

Methods

The data are drawn from a longitudinal study of one age-group of London children. The first phase took place in 1970, when the children were 10, and included all children then attending local authority primary schools in one inner London borough (n = 2281). A survey of this complete sample was complemented by a more intensive study of randomly selected sub-groups of both black and white children. The first follow-up reported here took place four years later, when the children were 14, and in their third year of secondary school. Attempts were made to trace all members of the original sample at this stage, including those who had moved out of London in the interim. A second stage of the study then followed an overlapping sample, all still in London secondary schools, up to the time they left school.

The children's ethnic background was determined on the basis of teacher reports of the place of birth of each child and both of his/her parents. The white group were children with both parents born in the UK or Eire, or one parent in the UK or Eire and the other in the USA, Australia, New Zealand or on the European mainland. In both

Barbara Maughan and Graham Dunn

Table 1:   Longitudinal sample

	White	Black	
		UK Born	Born abroad
Girls	666	91	61
Boys	701	94	52
All	1367	185	113
Percentage of original 10-year-old sample	80.9	88.9	77.4

parts of the study, approximately three-quarters of the total samples were white (in the 10-year-old sample, n = 1689, 74.1 per cent). The largest ethnic minority group consisted of children both of whose parents had been born in the West Indies (n = 354, 15.5 per cent of the 10-year-old sample). Within this black group, almost 60 per cent of the pupils (n = 207) were reported as born in England, while the remainder had come to this country at some point in their childhood. We have no more precise details of the ages at which the children arrived in the UK.

The first two phases of the study involved the administration of group reading tests, of the sentence completion variety, which tapped comprehension and vocabulary skills. At age 10, the test was the NFER SRA and at 14 the NFER NS6. Both tests have standard scores ranging from 70 to 140. Table 1 shows the Ns in each sub-group of pupils with test data from both occasions, and the proportions of the original sample with full longitudinal data in each ethnic group. The losses reflect a combination of failure to trace some members of the sample at 14, and absences from the testing. The slightly higher rate of losses amongst black pupils born abroad was largely accounted for by a small number of children who had left the UK since the first stage of the study. In general, however, the follow-up rate was relatively high in all groups.

Results

As a background to the analyses of progress over the early secondary school years, table 2 shows results from the initial testing when the children were in their fourth year at primary school. In this inner city sample, average scores for the white children were rather below national norms, and results for the black pupils followed the trends found in other research: black children born abroad had the most

114

Table 2: *Reading scores at age 10*

| | White | | Black | | | |
| | | | UK born | | Born abroad | |
	$\bar{X}$	sd	$\bar{X}$	sd	$\bar{X}$	sd
Girls	96.72	(13.90)	91.13	(11.93)	83.39	(9.40)
Boys	94.70	(15.50)	86.93	(12.67)	83.00	(11.42)
All	95.68	(14.77)	88.99	(12.46)	83.21	(10.33)

Table 3: *Transformed reading scores at 10 and 14*

| | | | Reading scores | | |
			Age 10	Age 14	Difference
Girls:	All		0.069	−0.008	−0.077
	White		0.178	0.082	−0.096
	Black:	UK born	−0.201	−0.287	−0.086
		Born abroad	−0.727	−0.577	0.150
Boys:	All		−0.066	0.008	0.074
	White		0.041	0.116	0.075
	Black:	UK born	−0.487	−0.441	0.047
		Born abroad	−0.754	−0.636	0.119

depressed scores, but UK born black pupils were also reading well below the levels of whites. In general, at this age, girls' reading attainments were rather better than boys'.

Progress Between 10 and 14

To explore progress over the early secondary school years, scores from both testings were transformed into standard deviation units from the sample mean. Table 3 shows these transformed scores at each testing, together with a simple difference measure for each sub-group of pupils. Figure 1 displays the results graphically. Focussing first on the results for the white children, it is clear that over this particular age span, the slight advantage in reading in favour of girls noted at 10 was reversed by the age of 14. This is a frequently reported trend in studies of reading attainment in early adolescence, and seemed a potentially important background consideration to bear in mind in comparing the progress of black and white pupils.

Black pupils born abroad appeared to have improved their position to some extent over the period, while UK born black girls

Barbara Maughan and Graham Dunn

Figure 1:   *Transformed reading scores at 10 and 14*

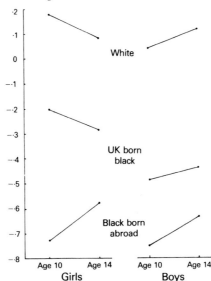

had clearly maintained similar rates of progress to whites. The only suggestion of any relative decline in performance within the black samples appeared to be for UK born black boys, whose progress was slightly less marked than that of white boys.

Analysis of covariance is probably the most widely used technique for analyzing progress data of this kind. Taking 14-year-old scores as the dependent variable, and 10-year-old scores as the covariate, we can assess how far any of the sub-groups differed in their rates of progress over the period. Initial analyses confirmed the sex effects suggested above, so the remainder of the analyses were conducted separately for boys and girls. For girls, a three group comparison contrasting white, UK born black, and black pupils born abroad showed no significant differences between subgroups in 14-year-old reading levels once 10-year-old scores had been taken into account (F = 1.28, df = 2,814, ns). For boys there was a trend (F = 2.79, df = 2,843, P = 0.062) for black pupils to have made slightly slower progress in reading between 10 and 14. Contrasting only UK born Black boys with whites, this trend reached statistical significance (F = 4.03, df = 1,792, P < 0.05). The adjusted mean for all Black boys was equivalent to just under two standardized points below that of whites, a small difference that would fall well within the standard error of measurement of the test. Our conclusions from these initial analyses would thus be threefold: first, that over the particular age-range studied here, it is important to take sex differences into account

116

in looking at progress in reading; second, that although black children born abroad had made some gains relative to the other two groups over the period, these promising results were not statistically significant; and third, that the analyses in general showed black pupils making essentially similar progress to whites. More detailed explorations might be needed before we could assess the importance of the trend towards slightly slower progress among UK born black boys.

Social Background and School Effects

With this general picture of the initial results in mind, we now go on to look at the effects of two sets of factors widely accepted as important in any discussion of minority group pupils' school progress: social background variables, and possible school effects. Even within our inner city sample, we knew that the black children in our study were more likely to have faced greater social disadvantages, in areas known to be associated with attainment in white populations, than their white peers. In the total 10-year-old sample, the parents of one fifth of the black children were in completely unskilled work, by comparison of only 13 per cent of white parents, while contrasts at the upper end of the SES spectrum were even more striking: only 4 per cent of black parents were in non-manual occupations of any kind, by comparison with 22 per cent of white (Yule *et al.*, 1975). The intensive phase of the 10-year-old study had highlighted many other differences between the groups. To take just a few examples, the black children were more likely to come from large families, and to live in overcrowded homes with poor facilities. Their pre-school experiences also differed, many more of the black children having been minded by adults outside their own families. Set against this, however, black parents' interest and concern for their children's education was quite as strong as that of whites' (Rutter *et al.*, 1975).

For the sample studied here, our social background indicators were restricted to the relatively crude measures frequently collected in large-scale surveys: parental occupation, and, as a more specific indicator of economic disadvantage, receipt of free school meals. We had intended to include these measures in the analyses, to assess how far our initial picture of progress in the different ethnic groups was affected by variations in these areas. It is only justifiable to do this, however, when the variables in question show the same relationships with the outcome measure in each of the sub-groups being compared. Inspection of our data showed this not to be the case here. Within the black groups, the associations between social indicators and attainment scores were much less consistent than for the white pupils, and in some instances actually went in quite the opposite direction from expectation. Where in a white population we are normally accustomed to take indicators such as socioeconomic status as reflecting a range of educationally-related attitudes and aspirations, as well as material conditions, this may be a less justifiable assumption in studies of minority groups. The reasons do not seem hard to seek: it is well known that many black adults are in low paid and relatively unskilled jobs, often quite incommensurate with their previous work experience or qualifications. In these circumstances, conventional indicators of social and economic status may not produce the socially meaningful groupings we have come to expect from much earlier research. This is not to argue, of course, that the social disadvantages that black children face do not contribute to their depressed performance, but instead, that somewhat more sensitive, and possibly different, indicators may be needed to reflect the processes involved. In the present study our only means of taking some account of social background differences was to repeat the analyses for children from broadly working class backgrounds in each ethnic group. When we did this, there were no significant differences in rates of progress between black and white pupils for either girls or boys. For children of broadly similar social circumstances, reading progress was quite as positive in black as in white groups.

On the question of school effects two rather different questions arose. The first concerned the broad type of secondary school the pupils attended. At the time of our research, some grammar schools still remained within the ILEA, but very few of the black children in our sample gained grammar school places (2 per cent by comparison of 13 per cent of whites). These differences in school experiences might have had some confounding effect on the initial pattern of our results. Because of the very small number of black children in grammar schools, our best means of assessing this was to repeat the analyses, excluding all grammar school pupils, and focussing on the great majority of the sample, pupils in non-selective schools. The results of these ANCOVAs were as for the initial analyses: once 10-year-old reading scores had been taken into account, there were no significant differences between the 14-year-old reading levels of black and white girls ($F = 0.11$, df = 1,685, ns) but the trend for slower progress amongst black boys remained ($F = 3.37$, df = 1,707, $P = 0.07$). When, however, we repeated the contrasts for working class pupils only, these group differences were eliminated.

Figure 2: *Reading scores at 10 and 14 at non-selective schools: girls*

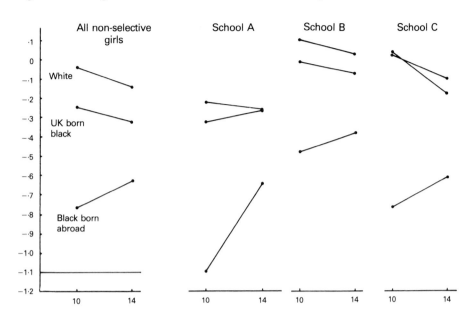

Our second concern under the broad heading of school effects was how far results at individual secondary schools reflected the pattern of the findings overall. It was possible, by pooling the data across schools, that we were in fact combining together results from individual schools that each showed very different patterns, and that our overall 'average' picture of progress was not typical of results at the school level. The pupils had of course dispersed to a large number of different secondary schools over the course of the study, and there were only a few secondary schools with large enough numbers of black pupils from the original sample for us to assess this. We were, however, able to look separately at results for each of five secondary schools that had admitted at least twenty black pupils from the original sample. These were all non-selective schools: three were single sex girls schools, one a single sex boys schools, and the last a mixed school. None of these analyses, whether for boys or girls, showed any significant differences in the rates of progress of black and white children within these schools. The numbers in some analyses were of course small, but these more detailed explorations failed to reveal any differences between the groups. Figure 2 illustrates the results for girls, showing the 10 and 14-year-old transformed scores for the three sub-groups of pupils at each school, set alongside the pattern for the total sample of girls at non-selective schools.

Although reading *levels* differed sharply between schools, the picture in each case was one of scores for UK born black pupils closely paralleling those of whites, and for some suggestions of more marked gains amongst the black pupils born abroad.

Later Secondary School Progress

Over the early secondary school years, then, our analyses showed black and white children making essentially similar progress in reading. A second phase of the study enabled us to explore whether this picture changed in any important ways when we came on to look at public exam results. Our sample here was a linked but slightly different one, which included all pupils in the age-group who attended twelve of the non-selective schools in the immediate area of the original study (see Rutter *et al.*, 1979). For all these pupils (n = 1768 white and 250 black), we had assessments of verbal reasoning at 11, reading test scores and attendance figures at 14, and results in all public exams up to the time the pupils left school.

We can only summarize the results briefly here. Several different features emerged. When we compared 16 year-old (fifth year) exam results for black and white pupils, the picture closely resembled that from other similar studies of this period. Black pupils were underrepresented in the highest achievement grades, and instead their results tended to group in the middle of the range (see figure 3). A second important difference between the groups, however, was that black pupils were much less likely than whites to reach compulsory school-leaving age without achieving at least some graded examination results. This seemed largely to reflect their much greater participation in the exam system, at both this fifth year stage and later. Table 4 shows school-leaving dates for pupils in both groups. It is clear that black pupils were less likely to leave school early, before sitting exams, and also that girls in particular were more likely to stay on into the sixth form to continue their studies. This greater investment in schooling had been evident much earlier in their secondary school careers: black pupils' attendance had been significantly better than whites' at 14 (96.3 per cent by comparison with 89.9 per cent), and continued to be significantly higher through to the fifth year.

Two questions then remained. First, if we returned to our earlier concern with progress, did the fifth year results suggest similar rates of progress for black and white groups given their earlier attainment levels? And second, how did the black pupils' greater exam participa-

Figure 3:   5th year examination results

GIRLS

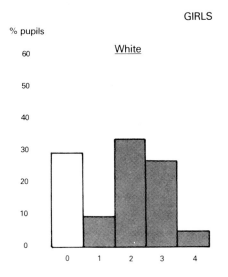
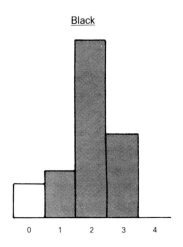

BOYS

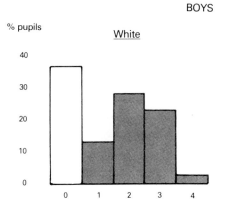
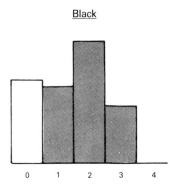

0 No graded pass
1 CSE 4 and 5 only
2 CSE 2 and 3, O level D and E
3 1-4 O level equivalents
4 5+ O level equivalents

Table 4: School leaving dates

| | Girls | | | | Boys | | | |
| | White | | Black | | White | | Black | |
	%	(N)	%	(N)	%	(N)	%	(N)
Easter fifth year	14.0	(107)	3.2	(4)	19.6	(197)	12.0	(15)
Summer fifth year	61.8	(472)	52.0	(65)	64.5	(648)	69.6	(87)
First year sixth	16.8	(128)	33.6	(42)	9.6	(96)	12.0	(15)
Second year sixth	7.5	(57)	11.2	(14)	6.3	(63)	6.4	(8)
Total		764		125		1004		125

Table 5: Fifth year exam attainments: candidates only

| | Mean examination score | | | |
| | Girls | | Boys | |
	White	Black	White	Black
VR band 1	23.33	24.83	21.54	22.00
VR band 2	15.46	15.33	13.45	10.58
VR band 3	6.73	11.16	6.73	5.29
All pupils:	15.04	13.47	13.21	8.41

tion affect the picture overall? On the first question, we assessed fifth year exam results (using a weighted scoring system to produce a continuous measure) against the background of 11-year-old VR scores and 14-year-old reading test results. Table 5 shows average exam scores for black and white exam candidates, broken down according to three broad VR bands at age 11. It is clear that there were only minor and inconsistent differences between groups. More detailed analyses against the background of 14-year-old scores showed significant sex differences, (F = 41.59, df = 1,1465, P < .001), but no differences between ethnic groups (F = 1.21, df = 1,1465, n.s.). For any given level of earlier attainment, black and white exam candidates achieved essentially similar results. This picture was the same at the sixth form level: black and white pupils entering the sixth form with comparable results made similar rates of further progress.

But we have already seen that black pupils, and especially black girls, were much more likely to stay on at school to take further exams and improve their earlier grades. If we focus on the total sample, rather than just those pupils who were exam candidates at any particular stage, we find that this greater persistence of the black groups resulted in some convergence in results for the two groups by the time of school-leaving, with the black pupils attaining rather better final exam scores than would have been predicted on the basis of their earlier attainments. This is most clearly illustrated by comparing the final school-leaving results of pupils in each ethnic group (figure 4). Assessing these final leaving results against the background of the pupils' earlier attainments, black pupils had achieved rather higher exam scores than whites, while the earlier pattern of sex differences remained. We should reiterate here that this sample was all drawn from non-selective schools. This had the advantage that we were comparing pupils with generally similar school and curriculum opportunities, rather than, as often happens, contrasting ethnic group results for pupils whose school experiences have varied widely. By omitting grammar school pupils, most of whom were white, we have of course focussed on a restricted sample; comparisons with a more fully representative white group would almost certainly have shown the black pupils at a greater disadvantage. It is equally important to recall, however, that these black pupils were assessed as attaining much less well on average when they entered secondary school than white children in the same schools. Their relative 'success' by the time of leaving school owed much to their greater involvement and persistence in secondary education throughout.

Some Statistical Problems

We conclude with some more general comments on the statistical problems encountered in a study of this kind. Anyone who has ever seriously attempted to analyze the results of a longitudinal survey such as this will be aware of the many pitfalls to be faced in interpreting the data. As we noted earlier, longitudinal data provide probably the best basis for contrasting the progress of 'intact' groups of pupils, but they nevertheless raise a series of issues that require careful attention before conclusions can be drawn. However thoroughly one looks at the data, however careful one is to avoid making unjustified claims, there is always the possibility that the conclusions reached after the analysis reflect statistical artefacts created by inadvertant bias. Such biases can arise in the initial selection of subjects, and in a longitudinal or follow-up study by differential drop-out rates. In a study such as our own, for example, the different populations may have differed in their rates of emigration from the study area in the follow-up period, making it more difficult for us to trace members of some groups rather than others. There will also be different rates of non-

Barbara Maughan and Graham Dunn

Figure 4:   Fifth year and final examination attainments

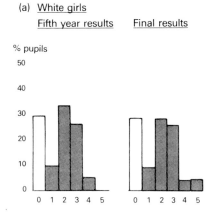

(a) White girls
     Fifth year results   Final results

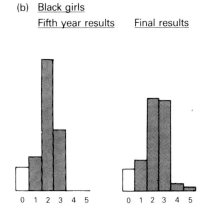

(b) Black girls
     Fifth year results   Final results

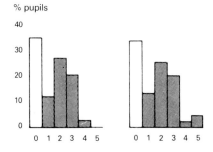

(c) White boys
     Fifth year results   Final results

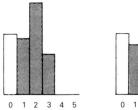

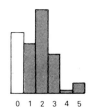

(d) Black boys
     Fifth year results   Final results

Key: 0 = No graded pass
       1 = CSE 4 or 5
       2 = CSE 2 or 3, 'O' level D or E
       3 = 1+ 'O' level equivalents
       4 = 5+ 'O' level equivalents
       5 = 1+ 'A' levels.

attendance from school among older pupils, again introducing possibilities of bias into the outcome results. The various sub-groups being studied will inevitably differ on a range of characteristics, likely to be related to outcome, that we are unable to represent fully in the analyses. Aspects of social disadvantage were the most obvious examples in the present study. How can one cope with these threats to the validity of the statistical conclusions? All we can do is try to identify all possible sources of bias, and then see if the results are stable when allowance is made for them in the statistical analyses. In the present study, our initial sample — of all children in the age group in local authority schools — should be as fully representative of black and white inner London pupils at this period as possible, and the follow-up rates in all groups were high. It is difficult to know how far the results would be generalizable to other areas or more recent periods (and indeed there is encouraging evidence that West Indian pupils' exam results have improved somewhat in recent years). Within the confines of our sample, however, we feel confident that none of these initial types of problems should pose major threats to the validity of the conclusions.

A second source of artefact, particularly in the study of a developmental process such as reading ability during schooling, is the lack of independence of the observations. Pupils in 'good' schools will be taught well, usually in groups, and they will make good progress. Pupils in poor schools will make slower progress. If we fail to take this into account, we may attribute aspects of the findings to group differences when they more properly reflect school effects. One way round this problem is to introduce a blocking or stratifying factor in an analysis of variance/covariance, to allow for school membership. Ideally, the analysis might be carried out using some sort of random-effects model (as opposed to fixed-effects). Alternatively, one can look at the performance of children within individual schools. The latter approach was adopted here.

Finally, in any study of behaviour such as reading performance, there is the problem of measurement error. Tests of reading ability are nowhere near perfect. In an attempt to control for selection biases, we looked at differences in reading ability at 14 after allowing for measured ability at 10 in the analyses of covariance. That is, our analyses were conditional on observed differences at the first assessment. Although this approach is more satisfactory than the analysis of simple improvement scores, it suffers from the disadvantage that it involves the assumption that the covariate (that is, performance at age 10) is measured without error. Clearly this is not true. A second difficulty is the existence of a floor score of 70 and a ceiling of 140 on the tests.

We have attempted to get round some of these problems through the use of linear-logistic models (see Maughan, Dunn and Rutter, 1985). This more conservative approach to the analyses, which allows us to look at progress at particular points in the range, showed no differences between black and white groups in improvements from poor to average reading levels, or from average to good, for either girls or boys. We could also have introduced a correction for test reliability in the interpretation of the analyses of covariance (see, for example, Cochran, 1983; or Plewis, 1986). For the present data sets, the use of more realistic statistical models diminished, or even eliminated, any observed group differences in rates of improvement.

So, what can we conclude from our analyses? First, there are several sources of artefact in the data, as there will be in any data of this type. Second, if we attempt to allow for sources of trouble then such group differences as we identified initially get smaller, or even disappear altogether. Outcome differences are considerably diminished if one does an analysis conditional on scores at the first assessment of reading ability. Much of the difference between UK born blacks and whites at both first and follow-up assessments is reduced if one allows for school membership rather than looking at pooled data. Group differences are further diminished if we acknowledge the poor reliability of the measures. The message is simple. The more one thinks about the data, the more realistic the statistical analyses become. If one merely carries out a crude analysis of pooled data using unrealistic assumptions about their quality, then one is asking for trouble. In the present case, having thought carefully about the quality of our own data, we feel justified in concluding that, conditional on performance at the end of primary school, reading ability at 14 has nothing to do with ethnicity in the groups studied here. We found no evidence that black children were progressively falling behind their white peers during the early years of secondary schooling; and from evidence provided by their subsequent examination results, there are clear indications that they are able, by persistence in education, to make up to some extent for their earlier educational disadvantages.

References

COCHRAN, W.E. (1983) *Planning and Analysis of Observational Studies*, New York, John Wiley.

MABEY, C. (1981) 'Black British literacy: A study of London black children from 8 to 15 years', *Educational Research*, 23, pp 83–95.

MACKINTOSH, N.J. and MASCIE-TAYLOR, C.G.N. (1985) 'The IQ question', in COMMITTEE OF ENQUIRY INTO THE EDUCATION OF CHILDREN FROM ETHNIC MINORITY GROUPS *Education for All*, (Swann Report) Cmnd 9453 chapter 3, annexe D, London, HMSO.

MAUGHAN, B., DUNN, G. and RUTTER, M. (1985) 'Black pupils' progress in secondary school — I. Reading attainment between 10 and 14', *British Journal of Developmental Psychology*, 3, pp 113–21.

MAUGHAN, B. and RUTTER, M. (1986) 'Black pupils' progress in secondary school — II. Examination attainments', *British Journal of Developmental Psychology*, 4, pp 19–29.

PLEWIS, I. (1986) 'Analyzing data from longitudinal comparative studies', in LOVIE, A.D. (Ed) *New Developments in Statistics for Psychology and the Social Sciences*, London, Methuen, pp 93–112.

RUTTER, M., MAUGHAN, B., MORTIMORE, P. and OUSTON, J., with SMITH, A. (1979) *Fifteen Thousand Hours: Secondary Schools and Their Effects on Children*, London, Open Books.

RUTTER, M., YULE, B., MORTON, J. and BAGLEY, C. (1975) 'Children of West Indian immigrants — III. Home circumstances and family patterns', *Journal of Child Psychology and Psychiatry*, 16, 2, pp 105–24.

TOMLINSON, S. (1983) *Ethnic Minorities in British Schools*, London, Heinemann.

YULE, W., BERGER, M., RUTTER, M. and YULE, B. (1975) 'Children of West Indian immigrants — II: Intellectual performance and reading attainment', *Journal of Child Psychology and Psychiatry*, 16, 4, pp 1–17.

10 Inner City Adolescents: Unequal Opportunities?

Ann Dawson

Introduction

This chapter relates to a project undertaken with a group of over 5000 secondary school pupils in the north west of England. The project involved measures of attainment, attitude and aspiration of which only the results relating to attainment are given here. The group of pupils involved ranged in age from 12 to 16 at the time of the field work, being then in the first, third or fourth year of their secondary education. The attainment measures, however, relate in every case to their results on standardized tests taken during the second term of their first year at secondary school.

The young people attended ten different comprehensive schools in a northern city and each year group represented just over 20 per cent of the whole year cohort attending maintained secondary schools within the city. The ten schools were purposely chosen to include both single sex and co-educational establishments and also to include as high a proportion as possible of the ethnic minority pupils at secondary school in the area. For this latter reason no voluntary aided schools nor schools sited in the more affluent suburbs of the city were included in the project.

The current research was instigated as a result of earlier work with pupils of West Indian origin which had concluded that, although such pupils were more committed to school than their white colleagues, they tended to be over-represented in the lower bands or streams of their secondary schools (Dawson, 1978a and 1978b). This conclusion raised the question of educational attainment by pupils of West Indian origin and, when it was found that no local data existed concerning such attainment, at any level of schooling, the local education authority agreed to support an investigatory survey.

The authority agreed to make available the results of standardized tests of reading, mathematics and non-verbal reasoning undertaken by all pupils in the city during their second term at secondary school. It was hoped that it would then be possible to devise a suitable method of classifying the pupils on the basis of their ethnicity and that this would then allow analysis of the 12+ attainment data in order to check the levels of attainment of not only pupils of West Indian origin but also those from Asian backgrounds relative to their white English peers.

A growing concern over the past decade about the level of educational attainment of school pupils from minority groups has led to research work, much of which was reported by Taylor (1981). This had indicated that differences in attainment seem to be related to differences in ethnicity and home background. A review of this research gave rise to the basic structure of the project, which was seen as an exploratory one designed to acquire further knowledge in a field which appeared at the time to be somewhat lacking in factual evidence.

The Research Model

The model used for the project, which involved measures of attitude and aspiration as well as attainment, is shown in figure 1. The central area covered by the research model is that of attainment. Attainment was chosen specifically, rather than the more inclusive 'achievement', as it was considered practicable, with a large sample, to use standardized attainment measures rather than to develop measures for a much wider range of factors, some more easily assessable than others, such as those recently suggested by Gardner (1984).

There has been extensive debate about the relative importance of internal and external factors on attainment, not least in the area of so-called 'intelligence' testing and it has proved, to date, impossible to disentangle the inter-relationship of what have been termed 'heredity' and 'environment'. Within the research model it is seen as inevitable that a whole range of factors, including internal genetically controlled individual characteristics, external influences from school and society, and individual environmental factors resulting from ascribed characteristics, will effect the level of attainment of school children at the age of 12.

In order to search for any statistically and educationally significant differences in test scores between groups divided on the basis of

Figure 1: Research model

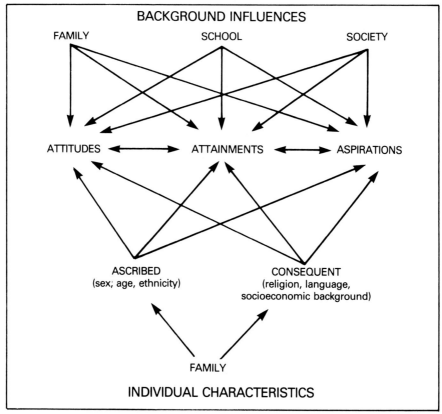

background and ethnicity, it was first necessary to produce suitable definitions and measures of these groupings.

Ethnicity

Within the society which is the multicultural Britain of the 1980s there are substantial numbers of ethnic minority group children in the educational system at both primary and secondary level. Some of these children, those whose skin colour is other than white, have what could be termed a 'high visibility index' and there has, consequently, been a danger that they might be grouped together as 'coloured' or 'immigrant' as different from the 'white indigenous' majority of the population. Davey (1983) notes in his recent research study that racial and ethnic distinctions are widely used by primary school children in the process of adapting to a multi-ethnic society and that, by the age of 7 or 8, children have not only learned the standard classification system but also what attitudes should be adopted towards people classified in a particular way. Children use classifications to simplify and make sense of the world in which they are growing up and they find their classificatory norms in the external, collective beliefs, stereotypes and prejudices of the world in which they grow up.

Differences in ethnicity are a basic fact of human existence, resulting from, at the least, 50,000 years of evolutionary change where groups living in relative isolation in geographically and climatically different areas have evolved adaptive physical characteristics to best suit their particular circumstances. This adaptive variation has given rise to human beings with demonstrably different colours of skin, texture of hair and facial structure, which in turn have led to various definitions of race. Geographical isolation has also given rise to groups who developed their own distinctive cultural norms, customs and religious beliefs. Physical and cultural differences combine to give overall differences in ethnicity so that, for example, on the Indian subcontinent there are major ethnic differences between various sub-groups. Such differences, however, are largely religious and cultural and so, to people with a different physical appearance, such as those from a northern European Celtic or Nordic group, the similarities in physical appearance of the two 'Asian' groups generally outweigh any differences in culture.

There is considerable semantic confusion between the terms 'race' and 'ethnicity', not least because physical appearance is a more obvious visible difference than is cultural background. Over a decade ago Allen (1971) wrote that

> the gap between scientific attempts at precise classification and everyday usage is wide when race is used in reference not only to biologically transmissable qualities but also to differences that are social in character. The confusion of religious, national and linguistic groups is scientifically incorrect.

This gap is still present and has become in some senses wider as the term 'race' has, in certain circumstances, begun to be seen as value judgmental, as indeed actually perjorative, and as, consequently, the term 'ethnicity' has begun to replace it in popular usage.

Within the project described here it was originally intended to use ethnicity, in its narrower sense, to describe a discreet group of people differentiated from other human groups by both physical and cultural factors. Awareness of the reality of the contemporary situation in Britain, however, led to a definition which, whilst using cultural background, language and religious belief as criteria, also acknowledged the overriding importance of physical appearance in the categorization of individuals by others.

Baughman (1971) noted that, for black Americans, it was social experience rather than biological difference which determined whether a person was considered to be 'black' or 'white' and that social definitions depended almost completely upon skin colour. The importance of skin colour and its link with social acceptance is also brought out by Davey's research (1983). In Britain children with a black skin, tightly curled hair and 'negroid' facial features are generally categorized by white skinned Britons as either 'Black' or 'West Indian'. Similarly those with brown skins, straight black hair and 'aryan' facial construction are generally termed 'Asian', 'Pakistani' or, more perjoratively, 'immigrant'. As a corollary to such gross classification, individuals with a white skin are generally labelled and treated as 'British' unless on closer acquaintance accent indicates that they are, for example, of Irish or Polish origin.

In Britain as a whole the current estimate of the 'black' population, mainly people of Asian or Afro-Caribbean ethnic origin, is around 3.5 per cent of the total population. About half of the present adult population of Asians and West Indians had settled in Britain before 1962 when, for the first time, entry was restricted by the Commonwealth Immigrants Act. It is estimated that by 1976 approximately 40 per cent of the total black population had been born in Britain (Davey, 1983). Since most of the immigrants to Britain from the so-called 'New Commonwealth' were young people, it is to be expected that the proportion of children born in Britain to members of these ethnic minority groups will have increased since that time. The 'black' children involved in the present work, being 12, 14 and 15 years old in 1981 will be expected, at the least, to have spent their school years in Britain and are likely to include a majority of British born adolescents.

It was considered inappropriate to describe the white majority group of pupils involved in the research as 'British' and so, to differentiate them from the British pupils of Asian or Afro-Caribbean origin, they are classified as of 'European' origin. This classification allowed the inclusion of white children from other areas of Europe, albeit few in number, who it was felt would, on physical criteria, be generally seen as 'white' and hence, in general parlance 'British'. The three classificatory groups used in the work were reflective of the way in which pupils would be viewed and, hence, treated by the general population rather than of the specific cultural, linguistic and religious background of each child.

When the project was initiated the prevailing 'climate', both politically and educationally, was such that it was seen as unwise to involve school staff in classifying pupils in any way relating to ethnic origin. It was also seen as inadvisable to include within the project questionnaire any direct question on ethnic group membership, or place of birth. This meant that a method had to be devised to ascertain ethnic group membership which was acceptable to pupils, teachers, LEA staff and ethnic minority group leaders, and which would also differentiate accurately between groups.

Considerable discussion followed with ethnic minority leaders, staff involved in 'multicultural education', and minority group adolescents themselves. As a result of this discussion it was decided to structure a group of questions which, when taken together, would give an accurate indication of the ethnic group membership, as perceived by the pupils themselves, of each adolescent involved in the project.

Each pupil was required to indicate whether s/he felt that they belonged to a country other than England, belonged to a special group, used a home language other than English and/or had a particular religious affiliation. The answers given to these questions were checked with each pupil's report of physical appearance, particularly skin, hair and eye colouring, and then with the individual's name before each pupil was grouped as African, Asian, Caribbean, Chinese, European or Black British.

When the project questionnaires were coded and analyzed it was found impossible to classify ninety-three pupils (1.8 per cent of the group) on these criteria, largely because their answers to the various questions proved incompatible with each other.

The European background pupils formed 72.6 per cent of the whole sample whilst African and Far Eastern groups accounted for only 0.5 per cent and 0.8 per cent respectively. Of the pupils from Asian and Caribbean backgrounds it is of interest to note that a higher proportion of the Caribbean background pupils saw themselves as 'Black British' than did those of an Asian background. The pupils with a Far Eastern background and those whose ethnic background could not be assessed accurately were not included in the main analysis.

With these two groups excluded, it was found that the groups describing themselves as 'Black British' rather than 'Asian' or 'Caribbean' responded no differently to the attitudinal and aspirational sections of the project than their peers who saw themselves, for example, as 'Pakistani' or 'Jamaican'. Hence five of the remaining groups were

Ann Dawson

combined to give 'Asian' and 'Afro-Caribbean' classifications which, with the 'European' group provided the major ethnic subdivisions for the research.

Thus much of the data analysis was concerned with a group of 5082 pupils, from three school year groups, with 72.6 per cent having a European cultural background, 12.5 per cent an Afro-Caribbean one and 12.2 per cent an Asian one. Within the year groups the proportion of pupils from non-European backgrounds rose slightly from fourth year to first and the proportions of the two minority ethnic groups also changed, with a growing number of pupils from Asian backgrounds and a decreasing number from Afro-Caribbean ones. Within this latter pattern, however, the third year group included the highest number of Afro-Caribbean pupils (14.4 per cent).

'Background'

It was also felt that the characteristic of 'family background' should be obtained by combining the answers to a number of specific questions rather than simply relating this to the socioeconomic class of the father. A number of authors had already indicated that a much wider range of influences could affect pupils' attitudes and achievements (Wiseman, 1964; Sumner and Warburton, 1972; Batten 1974). Additionally, it seemed likely that a considerable number of pupils in the sample would come from homes where the mother was the main wage earner, where both parents were unemployed, or indeed from 'one-parent' families where to base a background measure solely on father's occupation could be both hurtful and misleading.

A composite 'background' variable was, therefore, designed using the reports given by each pupil of family size, number of siblings still at home and/or school, educational background of both parents and siblings and occupation (where applicable) of both father and mother.

The composite measure was then sub-divided into three levels which were named 'advantaged', 'average' and 'disadvantaged'. In the context of the sample, a pupil of average background might be described as from an urban working class family, with one or both parents in semi- or unskilled jobs, and having one or two siblings, who might possibly be involved in further education at a local college.

An 'advantaged' pupil, by the same measure, would have at least one parent in a higher clerical or professional occupation, one or two siblings, and either or both parents and siblings with experience of higher education, possibly at university level. A pupil with a relatively disadvantaged background would have either one parent working in an unskilled job or both parents unemployed and would be likely to belong to a larger than average family and to have no one in the family either studying or having studied in further or higher education.

The responses to questions relating to family background are given, in simple percentage terms, in table 1. As the figures have been rounded to the nearest whole number the total for each group is not always exactly 100 per cent.

In this context table 1 indicates that the pupils of Asian background are relatively more disadvantaged than their peers from either Afro-Caribbean or European backgrounds. Whilst just over half of each ethnic group might be described as of average working class background, over a third of the Asian pupils are relatively disadvantaged, compared with less than a quarter of those from the other two groups. The Afro-Caribbean pupils, in turn, appear to be very slightly disadvantaged relative to the European ones.

It may seem unusual that the Afro-Caribbean pupils are no more disadvantaged than their European peers but this could well be explained by the research concentrating on an inner urban area where the relative level of deprivation of all inhabitants is quite high. Here ethnic minority pupils are being compared not with the whole of the white population of Britain but only with those remaining in the less 'attractive' inner city area.

The fact that the Asian pupils are relatively much more disadvantaged could be due to a number of factors, including the tendency for families to be larger and for a higher proportion of parents to be unemployed and this despite the fact that a higher proportion have been involved in study at a university or polytechnic than is the case for Afro-Caribbean or European parents.

There is an overall trend for the proportion of relatively advantaged pupils to increase slightly from first to fourth year at the expense of both of the other background groups. In that the composite variable uses as one of its factors a measure of family dependency this might, to an extent, be expected since, as the pupils themselves become older they are more likely to have older brothers or sisters in employment, or at college, and both parents are also more likely to be working outside the home. The only exception to this trend appears with the Afro-Caribbean pupils where the third year group includes slightly higher proportions of average and disadvantaged groups than might be expected.

Ann Dawson

Table 1: HOME BACKGROUND: an overall profile of the sample by ethnic group.

Measure	Whole sample n = 4,959 (%)	Asian n = 633 (%)	Afro-Caribbean n = 654 (%)	European n = 3,785 (%)
FAMILY SIZE				
One child	5	1	3	6
Two or three children	47	23	24	54
Four or more children	48	76	73	40
FAMILY DEPENDENCY				
All children in education	56	63	39	59
At least one child working	31	16	30	32
At least one child unemployed	14	21	31	10
EDUCATIONAL BACKGROUND				
At least one family member attended university/polytechnic	10	14	8	10
At least one family member attended college of FE	36	37	57	33
Involved in FE or HE				
Parents	14	14	14	14
Siblings	32	37	51	29
FATHER'S OCCUPATION				
Professional/technical	12	19	3	12
Clerical/service	11	10	11	11
Skilled manual	26	21	25	27
Semi- & unskilled manual	23	18	20	25
Unemployed	24	31	36	22
MOTHER'S OCCUPATION				
Professional/technical	9	3	19	8
Clerical/service	19	10	10	23
Skilled manual	9	7	13	9
Semi- & unskilled manual	23	5	17	27
Not in paid employment	39	74	39	32
OVERALL MEASURE OF HOME BACKGROUND				
Advantaged	19	13	20	20
Average	57	52	55	57
Disadvantaged	24	34	25	23

The differences in overall home background can, to an extent, be explained by the differences found in the various components of the variable. Whilst ordinal position (not shown in table) is not in itself used to help determine overall background, it indicates certain differences between the ethnic groups. A considerably lower proportion of the Afro-Caribbean pupils, for example, are the eldest children in their family than is the case for either Asian or European groups and, as a corollary, a larger proportion have two or more older siblings. There is thus a tendency in the sample for the Afro-Caribbean pupils to come from families of relatively older children and this is likely to affect their overall background.

Family size adds to the details given by ordinal position the information that pupils of both Asian and Afro-Caribbean background are much more likely to belong to families with four or more children than are those of European background. This also confirms, however, the difference between the European families involved in this project and those of the population as a whole as almost 40 per cent of the sample families have four or more children. Differences between the sexes and the year groups are very slight on this measure.

Family dependency is essentially a measure of the economic involvement of siblings within the families to which the pupils belong. Overall about half of the pupils are from families where all children are under 16 years of age, almost one-third have an older sibling in employment whilst almost 14 per cent have an older sibling who has left school but who is out of work. There are some differences between year groups, with the proportion of families with children all of school age or younger decreasing from first to fourth year, as might be expected, whilst the proportion with at least one child working increases at a similar rate. At the same time the proportions with experience of an older sibling being out of work increase noticeably, more than doubling from first year to fourth and providing some indication of the growing problem of youth unemployment. There seems to be no obvious explanation for the finding that first year pupils are three times as likely to have an older sibling at college than are pupils from either the third or fourth year.

As with the measures already discussed, there are considerable differences between the ethnic groups. The Afro-Caribbean families show by far the highest proportion (31 per cent) of youth unemployment. The Asian families also suffer this to a greater extent (21 per cent) than the European ones (10 per cent). The Asian pupils have fewer older siblings in employment than do the other two groups and this, in part, confirms the impression that the Asian children come, on the whole, from younger families, although the proportion with all children of school age is very similar to that of the European group. The Afro-Caribbean pupils, conversely, have the lowest proportion of wholly school-age families and this again confirms the picture given by earlier measures of their being generally the younger children of the family.

Perhaps the most disturbing information in this table is that confirming the high incidence of youth unemployment reported in ethnic minority families.

Both Asian and Afro-Caribbean families are more likely to have unemployed siblings than is the case with European families and, additionally, in Afro-Caribbean households the mother is much more likely to be the only person in employment than is the case with the other two groups.

As might be expected from religious and cultural differences between the groups, it is unusual for Asian mothers to be in paid employment and hence also relatively unusual for both parents to be employed. Consequently Asian fathers are three times as likely to be the only family member in paid employment than is the case with either European or Afro-Caribbean groups.

There are only minor differences between the year groups or the sexes in terms of family economic involvement, with fourth years generally being the most likely to have siblings already at work and consequently the least likely to have only one or both parents working.

Two sections of the table give further details of family socioeconomic background through the actual occupations of both father and mother. The problem of unemployment is again highlighted, both overall in the area and, particularly, for the ethnic minority groups. Almost one quarter of the families in the sample have father out of work, rising to almost 36 per cent for the Afro-Caribbean families and 31 per cent for the Asian families. These figures will almost certainly be slightly higher than those prevailing in reality because of including more than one child from some families in the research but they are unlikely to be so distorted as to give a false picture of the relative levels of unemployment. The Afro-Caribbean fathers are noticeably underrepresented in the professional and technical occupational classes; Asian fathers, conversely, are well represented in this area and this may well reflect the number of Asian families involved in running their own small businesses. Asian men are relatively under-represented in all other occupational categories, having the lowest proportions of the three groups in either clerical or manual occupations. In these latter occupational classes the proportions of Afro-Caribbean men come between those of Asian and European backgrounds in each case.

There are few noticeable differences between the year groups in terms of father's occupation other than that first year pupils are more likely to have fathers in manual occupations or out of work than are older pupils.

Overall some 3 per cent of the pupils reported that they did not know their father's occupation, a figure which rose to 5 per cent for the Afro-Caribbean pupils. Pupils were less likely (1 per cent) to have doubts about their mother's occupation. Overall almost 40 per cent of the mothers were full time housewives and, of the rest, the majority were either in semi or unskilled jobs or involved in clerical or service work. Only 9 per cent were in skilled manual occupations, contrasted with 26 per cent for men in the sample, and 9 per cent in professional or technical ones, 12 per cent for the men. These figures would appear to reflect the general differences between male and female occupations fairly accurately.

There are few differences between the year groups. The percentage of full time housewives falls from first to third year but rises again in the fourth year group; the percentage of semi or unskilled workers is lowest in the fourth year group whilst those in the professional, technical and skilled manual categories rise with this group.

The most marked differences occur between the three ethnic groups. The Afro-Caribbean group has by far the largest percentage in professional and technical occupations, reflecting the number of Afro-Caribbean women employed in the nursing and paramedical fields; this group also includes the highest percentage of mothers with skilled manual jobs. The European group has the highest percentage of mothers employed in clerical, service and semi or unskilled manual jobs. Finally, as might be expected, the Asian group has by far the highest percentage of the three groups with mothers in the role of full time housewife and the lowest percentage in each of the other occupational divisions.

The final factor used to define the composite home background variable is that of the educational background of the pupil's family, and is based upon the attendance of any member of the immediate family at either college of further education, polytechnic or university. More than a third of the whole sample reported that at least one member of the family had studied at a further education college, undertaking a vocationally based course in preparation for work. The percentage reporting this rose steadily from first to fourth year, as might be expected with membership of an increasingly mature family group; there was very little difference between the responses of the sexes whilst the Afro-Caribbean group reported the highest percentage attendance at college amongst the ethnic groups.

Attendance by a family member at polytechnic or university was reported by almost 10 per cent of the sample, a proportion which varied very little between the year groups or the sexes but which showed notable variation between ethnic groups, with the Asian pupils reporting the highest and the Afro-Caribbean group the lowest percentage attendance.

A small proportion (6 per cent) of each group, divided by year, sex or ethnicity, reported that both parents had studied at college, polytechnic or university but, otherwise, fathers were more likely to have been involved than mothers. In every case more than 45 per cent of the pupils who reported any family involvement in post-school education stated that siblings had been the ones to attend. Between the various groupings there was, again, an increasing percentage involvement from first to fourth year, a virtually equal percentage of boys and girls, and noticeably high proportions of Asian and Afro-Caribbean pupils reporting sibling involvement in further or higher education. At the same time the Afro-Caribbean group reported the lowest percentage of parental involvement in higher education of any kind.

The responses relating to these different areas of home background were then weighted and combined to give the overall measure shown at the bottom of table 1. Although this table does not divide the pupils by year group or by sex it was, in fact, found that there was a slight, but noticeable, change in the proportions of relatively advantaged, average and disadvantaged family backgrounds for pupils from first to fourth year, as the pupils and their siblings become older, as mothers return to work, as siblings become involved in higher education or employment the proportion of relatively advantaged pupils increases and that of those who are relatively disadvantaged decreases. There were very slight differences on the measure for boys and girls, with girls somewhat more disadvantaged than boys.

When the ethnic groups are compared, the Asian group is shown to be relatively much more disadvantaged than the other two groups. It would seem likely that this fact might be due in part to the occurrence of predominantly larger and younger families, in part to the cultural norms which discourage most Asian women from taking work outside the home and in part to the relatively high rate of unemployment amongst Asian fathers. Some of these factors would, however, be counter-balanced by the relatively high level of involvement of Asian parents in higher education.

Without this latter factor it is likely that the Asian group would have appeared even more disadvantaged relative to the other ethnic groups. By contrast the Afro-Caribbean group, although slightly more disadvantaged than their European peers, are much less so than the Asian pupils. This may be explained, in part, by the greater proportion of pupils who were the youngest children in a family, thus being likely to have older siblings in further education or employment, and in part by the high percentage of Afro-Caribbean mothers in nursing or skilled manual occupations. These relative advantages would, however, be counterbalanced by the high level of unemployment amongst Afro-Caribbean fathers and young people as well as by the relatively low status of most fathers' occupations or educational backgrounds.

The members of the majority, European, group may also be seen to be relatively disadvantaged when compared with a whole city sample as most had larger than average families and suffered from higher than average levels of unemployment. It has to be borne in mind, when considering any effects resulting from differences in home background, that an 'average' classification within this project is used to describe what might be termed an urban working class family of two or three children with the pupil's parents and/or siblings in clerical or manual occupations and, perhaps, some family involvement in vocational training at a college of further education.

Measures of Ability and Attainment

The policy of the local education authority has been to organize the standardized administration of tests of reading, mathematics and non-verbal reasoning to all pupils in maintained schools at the ages of 7+, 10+ and 12+.

Tests of reading and mathematics are generally accepted as valid indicators of in-school attainments, as measures of the concepts and skills which depend upon direct instruction and on the child's interest and industriousness in the particular subject tested. The tests used by the LEA are provided by NFER and were administered to all pupils in the survey during the second term of their secondary education.

Tests of verbal or non-verbal reasoning, sometimes known as 'intelligence' or 'IQ' tests, are essentially designed as measures of ability, as a basis from which to assess a child's potential for school based learning. There has been considerable debate in recent years over the value of such tests, particularly in relation to children from minority ethnic groups. The question has been raised as to whether these tests actually measure potential or performance, whether they reflect innate ability or rather a combination of this with experience, thus being dependent on prior learning and hence on the opportunity for such learning.

Studies of verbal reasoning tests in particular have produced the possible conclusion that 'verbal IQ' as such may not be a very useful measure, particularly for children of West Indian origin. The scaling of verbal IQ tests is seen as maximizing the difference between individuals rather than concentrating on the cognitive skills shared by all individuals. Most workers find fewer problems with measures of non-verbal reasoning although it seems probable that the generally lower scores obtained by children of West Indian origin on these tests are far more likely to arise from cultural differences, language handicap or even emotional difficulties than to be indicators of an innately low potential ability.

In discussing measures of ability and attainment Taylor (1981) emphasizes the difficulties of finding appropriate and meaningful methods of assessment in a multicultural context. She also discusses the view initiated by Jensen that black children are genetically of lower intelligence than white and states that he appears to have reached 'premature conclusions on inadequate evidence' (p. 49). She notes that, whilst there may be a genetic component to IQ differences, it is certain that environmental factors account for some of the differences found between groups.

Taylor's argument here points up the dangers inherent in any comparison of group means with present tests of ability. It is perhaps appropriate to note that, although relatively small scale work is being undertaken to develop culture fair testing methods, following the work of Haynes (1971) and Hegarty and Lucas (1978), older ability tests designed for middle class white children continue to be used in schools. Whilst such tests are still in use it would seem better to view them as indicators of 'readiness for education' than as measures of innate ability or 'intelligence'. Such readiness for education would not depend upon the concepts and skills specifically taught in schools but upon those internalized by children as they develop through infancy and childhood and would thus, of necessity, be dependent upon cultural and socioeconomic background.

Thus, for example, the studies noted by Taylor relating to non-verbal reasoning tests, which are often referred to, somewhat loosely, as 'intelligence tests', and which all indicate a significantly lower mean score for children from ethnic minority groups than that obtained by indigenous white children might be seen as indicating simply a lack of preparedness for English education on the part of the non-white children.

When considering measures of attainment, that is those relating to the concepts and skills which depend upon teaching and upon the child's own interest and industriousness, Taylor notes that the common tools here are standardized tests of known reliability and validity. Again, most of the tests in use at present, including those concerned with reading skills and mathematics utilized in the present work, were designed and standardized for a population of indigenous white pupils and, moreover, for pupils from middle class rather than working class backgrounds.

Taylor notes that it is only recently that attention has been paid to the role of language for West Indian background pupils. Whilst most LEAs have rapidly implemented programmes in English as a Second Language (ESL) for pupils from Asian backgrounds there has been some reluctance to acknowledge the differences in syntax, pronunciation and general grammatical structure between West Indian Creole and 'standard' English and hence to extend some variant of the ESL programme to include pupils of West Indian origin.

It must, however, also be noted at this point that such reluctance is not wholly on the side of the educationalists for, since the speaking of standard English has been taken as an indicator of high social status in the Caribbean, many older West Indians find it difficult to accept that their children have difficulties with standard English.

The projects reported by Taylor which have used group administered reading tests similar to those in the present work all show pupils of West Indian origin performing less well than their white peers and, where these were included in the research, less well than their Asian background peers too. Even when allowances are made for home circumstances, the West Indian background pupil scores are still lower than the others.

Taylor reports that there is little information concerning mathematics attainment but that the larger scale studies (Little, 1968–75; BPPA 1978; Essen and Ghodsian, 1979) indicate that pupils of West Indian origin perform poorly when compared with their Asian background and white peers. The work of Essen and Ghodsian in particular is similar to that of the present study. They report that, on NFER maths tests, the West Indian background pupils had lower scores than their white counterparts even when background was controlled.

The reasons for the low scores of ethnic minority pupils seem to be so complexly interwoven that they prove difficult to classify although it seems possible that differences in cultural background and language, together with the socioeconomic deprivation common to most ethnic minority groups contribute to a large extent to the basic 'underpreparedness' of minority children for English education,

Furthermore the few research findings already published would seem to indicate that the special programmes developed for children from Asian backgrounds, which acknowledge their possession of a home language other than English and which endeavour to compensate for this fact, appear to be helping them to develop their potential within the educational system to a much greater extent than is at present possible for their peers from a West Indian background.

At the present stage of this debate about tests of ability it seemed sensible to accept the standardized NFER tests used by the LEA.

The results of all three NFER tests, standardized to a mean of 100 and standard deviation of 15, were made available by the LEA and incorporated into the research in the case of all those pupils who were still attending their original secondary school.

Results

A complete set of attainment scores was available for only 4594 of the pupils in the sample, partly because some pupils had been absent for one or more of the tests and partly because some pupils had changed schools between the time of taking the tests and that of completing the questionnaire. In the case of fourth year pupils, for example, there was a time gap of over three years between these two events. Nevertheless the sample represented 21 per cent of the secondary population in the city within the three years groups considered.

The scores of the sample population vary very little from those attained by all secondary pupils in the city, being slightly higher in mathematics and slightly lower in reading and non-verbal reasoning. The differences between the scores of boys and girls found within the sample also reflect those found over the whole city, with boys having higher mean scores in both mathematics and reading than girls. It would appear that the sample is reasonably representative of the secondary pupils within the city as a whole in terms of 12+ attainment test scores.

There was very little difference between year groups for the three measures. This is to be expected since all pupils completed the attainment tests at the same stage in their secondary school careers, during the second term of their first year. In this sense the analysis of attainment measures should be seen as cross-sectional rather than longitudinal, as representing a direct comparison between three age cohorts at a specific stage in their educational experience.

When the three major ethnic groups are considered differences in attainment scores are noticeable and statistically significant (table 2). Over the whole sample the Afro-Caribbean group has the lowest mean score on all three of the measures used. The actual differences in mean score between the Afro-Caribbean and European groups are about half of a standard deviation for each measure and so indicate a significant educational difference between group extremes moderated by a fairly high degree of overlap between the groups. The Asian pupils mean scores fall between those of the Afro-Caribbean and European groups in each measure. This general picture also applies to each of the year groups taken separately with only one exception; amongst first year pupils the Asian group has the lowest mean score on reading.

These results would seem to suggest that the Afro-Caribbean group in particular are relatively underprepared for secondary school education in Britain and have noticeable difficulties in both literacy and numeracy when compared with their white peers.

The Asian group, who might be expected to have the lowest mean scores in reading as most have a home language other than English, do not generally fare as badly as the Afro-Caribbean pupils although they do have lower scores than the European pupils. It seems likely that this is partially due to the ESL (English as a Second Language) programme organized by the local education authority for Asian pupils at both primary and secondary schools, a programme not generally available for Afro-Caribbean pupils who are assumed to have English as their home language.

The differences in non–verbal reasoning scores indicated in table 2 would appear to vindicate the decision to view these as measures of readiness for English education rather than as measures of innate ability or 'intelligence'. There is little to indicate that children of Asian or Afro-Caribbean descent are intrinsically less able than those of European descent and no less to support the idea that their cultural background is sufficiently different from that of the English pupils to disadvantage them to a greater or lesser extent in standardized tests.

An analysis of covariance was undertaken for the three ethnic groups within the whole sample. Whilst a caveat concerning background changes between year groups was acknowledged, it was felt that as the relative background changes were of the same order for all three groups the overall effect was unlikely to alter significantly any differences between the ethnic groups. Additionally, as all pupils had undertaken the attainment tests at the same stage in their school careers, it was felt to be more useful to treat this as a cross-sectional study and so maximize ethnic minority group representation. The

Table 2: *Analysis of variance over the attainment measures for the three major ethnic groups in the whole sample and within each year group*

GROUP	MEASURE	ASIAN		AFRO-CARIBBEAN		EUROPEAN		F	SIGNIFICANCE
		Mean	S.D.	Mean	S.D.	Mean	S.D.		
WHOLE SAMPLE n = 4499		n = 526		n = 566		n = 3407			d.f. 2/4496
	MATHEMATICS	100.8	12.7	96.0	11.7	102.5	12.4	23.4	<.001
	READING	96.0	11.0	95.5	11.7	100.5	13.0	22.2	<.001
	NON-VERBAL REASONING	99.9	12.4	96.9	12.2	102.4	13.0	19.6	<.001
FIRST YEAR n = 1589		n = 234		n = 174		n = 1181			d.f. 2/1586
	MATHEMATICS	101.1	12.8	98.8	12.6	102.7	12.4	8.1	<.001
	READING	95.8	11.6	97.3	11.1	100.6	13.0	17.0	<.001
	NON-VERBAL REASONING	98.7	12.5	97.8	12.3	102.4	13.1	15.5	<.001
THIRD YEAR n = 1503		n = 168		n = 214		n = 1121			d.f. 2/1500
	MATHEMATICS	101.8	12.5	94.9	11.7	102.4	12.5	33.2	<.001
	READING	95.6	10.9	95.1	11.9	99.9	13.4	17.8	<.001
	NON-VERBAL REASONING	101.9	12.6	97.0	12.5	102.8	13.3	18.0	<.001
FOURTH YEAR n = 1407		n = 124		n = 178		n = 1105			d.f. 2/1404
	MATHEMATICS	98.9	12.5	94.7	10.3	101.9	12.1	29.4	<.001
	READING	96.7	10.3	94.1	11.7	100.6	12.6	25.5	<.001
	NON-VERBAL REASONING	99.4	11.9	95.9	11.8	102.3	12.8	21.4	<.001

differences between the three ethnic groups on the measure of non-verbal reasoning remained much the same for Afro-Caribbean and European pupils when adjusted for differences in home background (table 3). This was to be expected as these two groups had similar home background distribution patterns. The mean score of the Asian group was affected to a greater extent because of the relatively disadvantaged home background of the Asian pupils (See table 1). The mean score of the Asian group, after controlling for home background, thus rose from 99.2 to 100.2. Nevertheless, even after such adjustment the Afro-Caribbean group mean score was half a standard deviation less than the European group mean score.

On the mathematics measure, unadjusted scoring showed the Afro-Caribbean group to have the lowest mean score and this relative position persisted when scores were adjusted for differences in home background and non-verbal reasoning score. With the latter factor as covariant the score differences were considerably reduced whilst the adjustment resulting from background differences was relatively slight. When background and non-verbal reasoning scores were taken simultaneously as covariants then the difference between the scores of the extreme groups fell to less than 15 per cent of a standard deviation. Whilst this difference remained statistically significant it could not be viewed as educationally significant.

Thus when individual differences, resulting from home background and other personal factors, were taken into account the score differences between the three ethnic groups on the mathematics test became educationally insignificant.

A slightly different pattern was shown by the unadjusted and adjusted reading scores. On the unadjusted scores the Afro-Caribbean group showed the lowest mean, almost half a standard deviation below that of the European group, with the Asian group score falling between these two extremes. When adjustment was made for home background differences the relative order of the mean scores remained unchanged but that of the Asian group was raised from 95.4 to 96.4. When non-verbal reasoning score was taken as covariant, however, the mean score of the Afro-Caribbean group was raised sufficiently to take it beyond that of the Asian group and to within 10 per cent of a standard deviation of the European group mean score, which had been decreased by the covariance adjustment. When both backgroud and non-verbal reasoning scores were used simultaneously as co-variants the differences between the three ethnic groups became statistically non significant.

Overall the analyses of covariance showed that when adjustments

Table 3: *Analysis of covariance over the attainment measures for the three major ethnic groups controlling for home background and non-verbal reasoning score differences. Whole sample n = 4,435*

MEASURE	MEAN VALUES	ASIAN	AFRO-CARIBBEAN	EUROPEAN	F	SIGNIFICANCE
MATHEMATICS	Unadjusted	100.8	96.0	102.5	23.4	<.001
	Adjusted for background differences	101.0	95.9	102.4	9.4	<.001
	Adjusted for differences in non-verbal reasoning score	102.1	99.2	101.7	7.6	<.001
	Adjusted for background and non-verbal reasoning score differences simultaneously	102.1	100.1	101.8	4.3	<.05
READING	Unadjusted	96.0	95.5	100.5	22.2	<.001
	Adjusted for background differences	96.4	95.4	100.5	16.0	<.001
	Adjusted for differences in non-verbal reasoning score	97.0	98.6	99.9	5.2	<.01
	Adjusted for background and and non-verbal reasoning score difference simultaneously	97.6	98.7	99.8	2.8	N.S.
NON-VERBAL REASONING	Unadjusted	99.9	96.9	102.4	19.6	<.001
	Adjusted for background differences	100.2	96.6	102.4	15.5	<.001

Note
The author and the editors recognize the restrictions involved in using analysis of covariance to deal with the data obtained. We are aware of the assumptions concerning the nature of the data that must be met if the technique is to be used. The data used here contain significant differences between ethnic groups on certain independent variables. Scores have been adjusted on the basis of non-chance variables. The argument for carrying out such exploratory analyses is that the analysis of covariance model is a robust one. In certain circumstances, some authorities consider that its use allows a rough ordering of the relative contributions of the variables to the overall discrimination on the dependent variable.

were made for differences in home background the Afro-Caribbean group continued to have the lowest mean scores in all three measures and the European group the highest mean scores. When adjustments were also made for differences in non-verbal reasoning score, however, the differences between groups were diminished to become barely or non significant in statistical terms.

The basic analyses thus confirmed results found in other parts of Britain which showed ethnic minority pupils to be under-attaining relative to their white peers. The analyses of covariance, however, would seem to hint that the reasons for such under-attainment relate to a considerable extent to the individual backgrounds of the minority group children.

Both home background scores, which might be seen as measures of relative deprivation, and non-verbal reasoning scores, which here are viewed as measures of relative preparedness for secondary education, have the effect of depressing scores on reading and mathematics for ethnic minority pupils. When these two measures are taken together the adjusted scores on reading and mathematics indicate that minority group pupils are in fact reaching a very similar level of attainment to that of their white peers in the particular inner urban environment studied here.

All the pupils in this survey could be seen as relatively deprived when compared with a countrywide sample and the ones from ethnic minority groups would appear to have an even greater hurdle to overcome before they have the opportunity to realize their full educational potential. It would seem that, unless positive steps are taken to look in detail at such deprivation and then to try to remedy it, a notable proportion of our secondary school pupils will continue to have what might be termed unequal opportunities.

Discussion

It has been suggested that minority group under-attainment could result from differences in home background, language, pre-school experiences, a clash between the values of home and school, inappropriate teacher training and school curriculum, negative teacher attitudes and expectations, and racism within British society, the research findings indicate that much of the variation in attainment, at least at 12+, is the result of individual rather than external factors. Amongst the many possible causes of under-attainment, the research emphasizes the importance of the home and of early childhood development as determinants of school attainment. From these results it would appear that minority group children are disadvantaged relative to their white peers by virtue of the cultural and socio-economic background of their homes, by the methods of communication used at home and by the forms of play and other pre-school experiences they had. These factors appear to be of much more importance than school curriculum, teacher training, attitude or expectation, clashes between home and school, alienation from parents or depressed levels of self-conceptualization (most of which were studied in the overall project).

The research also indicates the need to develop programmes of both pre-school experience and in-school support in order to allow children from the ethnic minority groups to attain their educational potential. It emphasizes the need to accept the inherent cultural differences between both Asian and Afro-Caribbean homes and those of the white majority of the population and to acknowledge these cultural differences in the preparation for and producing of tests of attainment.

References

ALLEN, S. (1971) *New Minorities, Old Conflicts*, New York, Random House.
BATTEN, E. (1974) 'A study of the relationships between some home environment variables and secondary school achievement', unpublished PhD thesis: University of Manchester, Department of Education.
BAUGHMAN, E.E. (1971) *Black Americans*, New York, Academic Press.
BLACK PEOPLE'S PROGRESSIVE ASSOCIATION AND REDBRIDGE COMMUNTY RELATIONS COUNCIL (1978) *Cause for Concern: West Indian Pupils in Redbridge*, Ilford, BPPA and RCRC.
DAVEY, A. (1983) *Learning to be Prejudiced*, London, Edward Arnold.
DAWSON, A.L. (1978a) 'The effect of sex and ethnic group on adolescent attitudes towards school and parents', unpublished MEd dissertation, University of Manchester.
DAWSON, A.L. (1978b) 'The attitudes of black and white adolescents in an urban area' in MURRAY, C. (Ed) *Youth in Contemporary Society*, Slough NFER.
DAWSON, A.L. (1984) 'Characteristics, attainments and attitudes of secondary school pupils of European, Asian and Afro-Caribbean descent', unpublished PhD thesis, University of Manchester.
ESSEN, J. and GHODSIAN, M. (1979) 'The children of immigrants: School performance', *New Community*, 1, 3, pp 422–9.
GARDNER, H. (1984) *Frames of Mind: Theory of Multiple Intelligences*, London, Heinemann.

HAYNES, J.M. (1971) *Educational Assessment of Immigrant Pupils*, Slough, NFER

HEGARTY, S. and LUCAS, D. (1978) *Able to Learn*, Windsor, NFER.

LITTLE, A. (1975) 'Performance of children from ethnic minority backgrounds in primary schools', *Oxford Review of Education*, 1,2, pp.117–135.

LITTLE, A., MABEY, C. and WHITAKER, G. (1968) 'The education of immigrant pupils in inner London primary schools', *Race*, IX, 4 April.

MURRAY, C. and DAWSON, A. (1984) *Five Thousand Adolescents*, Manchester, University of Manchester Press.

SUMNER, R. and WARBURTON, F.W. (1972) *Achievement in Secondary School: Attitudes, Personality and School Success*, Windsor, NFER.

TAYLOR, M. (1981) *Caught Between: A Review of Research into the Education of Pupils of West Indian Origin*, Windsor, NFER-Nelson.

WISEMAN, S. (1964) *Education and Environment*, Manchester, University of Manchester Press.

11 Self-Esteem and Educational Achievement in British Young South Asians

Gajendra Verma and Kanka Mallick

This chapter is part of a larger study concerned with educational, social, cultural and psychological processes which bear on educational performance for various ethnic groups in Britain. The main study was conducted in three phases during the period October 1977 to July 1983.

The first stage of research was designed to explore the determinants of the vocational aspirations, choices and achievements of South Asian adolescents in two major industrial cities in the North of England (see Verma, 1982 and 1983). The second stage examined the occupational experience of a cohort of adolescents containing a large proportion from the various ethnic minority groups, and attempted to set this experience in the context of achievement and expectations of working life. The final stage of research was concerned with the academic achievement of ethnic minority adolescents, and sought to establish profiles of high and low achievers among adolescents from differing ethnic groups.

There is a dearth of research, particularly the longitudinal type, which describes and interprets the various sociopsychological and cultural processes bearing on educational achievement for various ethnic groups. These processes represent complex interactions of many factors. It was necessary to develop an analytical model that would attempt to clarify how each factor operated within the whole process of adolescents' educational achievement. The findings of this research are reported elsewhere (Verma with Ashworth, 1986).

The variables — self-esteem and educational achievement selected for examination in this chapter were chosen for two main reasons. Firstly, many researchers have shown that self-esteem is associated with academic performance. Secondly, self-esteem was included in the main study both as a hypothetical precursor to examination success and occupation entry, and as one of the measures of educational achievement. It would seem necessary at this point to examine briefly the two concepts — self-esteem and educational achievement — as utilized in this chapter.

Self-Esteem and Achievement

Self-esteem has become an important vehicle in social science research for studying and understanding human behaviour. Although self-esteem is basically a social psychological concept it is also an important link between psychology and sociology (Weidman, 1969). It concerns the way an individual evaluates his/her personal characteristics. In theory, self-esteem differs from self-concept. Other terms such as 'identity', 'self-image', 'self-evaluation' and 'self-worth' are also used in the literature, sometimes interchangeably, but sometimes to imply different aspects of personality and personal functioning in social situations. For example, the terms self-esteem and self-concept refer to markedly different phenomena. Self-concept is the image or symbol which the individual has formed as a result of his or her personal experiences; self-esteem is the individual's evaluation of that image (Coopersmith, 1975). Thus self-esteem is an affective variable, involving an emotional appraisal of the 'self' whilst self-concept involved the recognition of one's characteristics, for example, one is married, white, tall and male. In many social situations self-concept plays an important part, for example in the recognition and denial of one's ethnicity. However, in most recent writings self-concept has been subsumed within the concept of self-esteem.

The literature on self-esteem has produced controversial findings. Earlier American studies tended to show that many black children had to a large degree internalized the negative stereotypes which the majority community held concerning them; in consequence they had poorer self-esteem than whites. More recent research with children and adolescents in America, however, has challenged this view showing that Blacks do not have significantly poorer self-esteem than whites (see Coopersmith, 1975; Bagley *et al.*, 1979). It would seem fair to say that the climate of ethnic minority self-esteem has clearly changed in the last ten years, and the possibility exists that the self-esteem of blacks in America may now be more positive than it was some years ago.

Studies in Britain of self-concept and self-esteem amongst ethnic minority pupils have also produced both diverse and contradictory findings. Our recent research (Verma with Ashworth, 1986) showed that the self-esteem of south Asian youngsters in Britain is in a state of transition. Their self-esteem norms fell somewhere between those found among English speaking, middle-class youngsters in India, and those among average British youngsters. Elements of both south Asian and British identity can be noticed in the self-esteem and identity of south Asian youth in Britain. Our findings of an earlier study (Bagley, Verma and Mallick, 1982) showed that South Asian young people in India are much more likely to evaluate themselves in a positive way than South Asian youngsters in Britain. However, this should not be taken to imply that south Asian youths in Britain have poorer self-esteem than their white peers. Other evidence indicated that levels of self-esteem are similar: that South Asian youngsters are acquiring bases of self-evaluation which are similar to those of white youths (Bagley, 1982).

It must be stressed that self-esteem is culturally grounded, and it is often meaningless as well as invidious to suggest that one ethnic group has 'better' self-esteem than any other. Self-esteem, as part of a more complex identity structure, has different groundings and different meanings in different ethnic groups. In a pluralistic framework of society, different ethnic groups have different psychological orientations; these have to be mutually understood and tolerated for successful, plural multiculturalism (Triandis, 1976).

The term 'achievement' has been interpreted in a variety of ways. In Britain the debate about the educational achievement of Asian and black pupils in schools, particularly those of Afro-Caribbean origin, has been the most controversial issue in the 'race and education' debate over the last decade or so. Much of the debate about why certain individuals or groups of individuals perform poorly centres on what the school is doing or not doing. Educational achievement is not simply the fulfilment of intellectual potential as measured by performance in public examinations. Such a criterion overlooks two important considerations. Firstly, educational achievement is the outcome of a complex process involving factors within an individual's environment. Secondly, public examinations are designed to cater for approximately 60 per cent of 16-year-olds, although perhaps as many as 80–85 per cent of them attempt examination entry in one or two subjects. Thus, examination performance itself is too simplistic a measure of educational achievement. For these reasons, four criteria of educational achievement were utilized in this research: public examination results, occupational entry, self-esteem and the youngster's satisfaction with his/her own education. This chapter is concerned with only one indicator i.e. self-esteem.

Self-esteem was included because there is considerable evidence that achievement and self-esteem are positively related (Simon and Simon, 1975; Prendergast and Binder, 1975) That is to say, those who perform less well, relative to their fellows, tend to have poor self-esteem. The relationship between below average achievement and poor self-esteem appears to hold in a comparative study of adolescents in America and Denmark (Weinland *et al.*, 1976).

In a multi-ethnic society, life affects not only the attitudes and behaviour of ethnic minority groups towards the standards set by the dominant group, but also the responses to themselves and their groups. The way the individual perceived himself is largely a product of his or her social experience with others (Verma and Bagley, 1979).

Some writers suggest that the relationship between pupil and teacher in the multi-ethnic classroom is a major factor which strongly influences the pupil's awareness of himself/herself (see Verma and Bagley, 1982). This awareness, once assimilated into the pupil's concept of himself/herself, becomes an influential element in learning (Purkey, 1978), and thus may operate as a significant factor in the low level of educational achievement. The findings of various studies summarized by Labenne and Greene (1969) indicate that poorly defined self-concepts or those which do not consider the fact that the pupil can gain increased competencies from his school experiences tend to result in under-achievement or poor performance. Studies have also shown that self-esteem is significantly related to educational achievement for disadvantaged as well as other pupils (Coard, 1971; Milner, 1975).

In our own study (Bagley, Mallick and Verma, 1979) we found that the most important structural correlations of the 'general-self' component of the Coopersmith Self-esteem Inventory (Coopersmith, 1967) were to be in a low stream at school, being of lower social class and being a sociometric isolate. The study concluded that in general, such a pupil has low academic achievement, is in a low stream and manifests various kinds of psychological maladjustment. Supportive peer groups can however counter adverse self-images which schools sometimes transmit — for example to ethnic minority adolescents (Bagley, Mallick and Verma, 1979).

Self-esteem may be defined as the assessment of the self-concept in positive or negative terms (Coopersmith, 1975). It is the picture an individual forms of himself or herself as a result of interacting with others within society. Self-esteem as a measure of academic achievement derives from an implicit aim of education, particularly for those who are seen as having low examination potential, that it must help the child to feel confident. Despite Stone's (1981) extensive critique of self-concept and self-esteem, it is true to say that the school whose pupils see themselves as potential successes rather than as academic failures could be said to be succeeding to some extent. Equally, the benefit to the individual of an education which helps pupils to understand themselves and the society in which they live cannot be altogether denied. Research evidence clearly shows that self-esteem is a crucial element in understanding an individual's personal, social and educational adaptation. Judging by the results of dozens of studies, mostly American, there seem ample support for the position that pupils who have more positive and definite appraisals of their ability to perform in school, and have more positive views of themselves do better in their academic work than those with more uncertain or negative views of themselves.

Patterns of South Asian Achievement and Self-Esteem

In the literature reference is frequently made to 'Asians' and 'West Indians' as ethnic groups. In such references there is an inherent danger of over-simplification since they tend to gloss over the complexities of 'Asian' and 'West Indian' society. Moreover, there is the danger with a particular geographical location — the area of origin of the group. The fact that two people come from the same sub-continent does not necessarily mean that they will behave in a more similar manner than two people who do not. Thus, classification of individuals by the sub-continent is most likely to hide ethnic, religious and cultural differences.

No studies to date have attempted to treat those from the Indian sub-continent as a non-uniform group; that is to say, existing studies have treated them as South Asian and have tended to ignore the important cultural and ethnic differences to be found amongst those whose origin lies in that broad geographical location. However, most of the available research suggests that, as a group, they perform at much the same level as the white population (Driver, 1977; Brooks and Singh, 1978; Verma, 1981). Such studies have compared South Asian youngsters with relatively disadvantaged white pupils. One explanation of the general parity between the educational achievement of South Asian youngsters and their white peers is that higher self-esteem amongst the South Asian group would seem to offset a position of 'multiple disadvantage'. Other researchers (Louden, 1980; Verma, 1981) also found that those of South Asian origin had a higher mean self-esteem than either West Indian or white adolescents. According to Coopersmith (1975) self-esteem represents an individual's appraisal of himself in positive or negative terms. It would seem almost inevitable that the social, familial, educational and personal experiences of an individual in respect of his or her cultural origins or skin colour have an effect upon his or her self-esteem, either positively or negatively. Thus, although the self-concept is a cognitive variable, self-esteem — the evaluation of that concept — is, in part, an emotional or affective dimension representing the cumulative effects of the environment as internalized by the individual. Hence self-esteem is a psychological variable through which socioeconomic and other external factors may be mediated. Verma (1981) explained his results of high self-esteem amongst South Asian youngsters by asserting that 'the adaptation processes of South Asians are mediated through the networks of family and friends, and to some extent through community based self-help systems'. Both Verma and Louden attributed the unexpectedly high self-esteem of South Asian adolescents to the immediate environment of the individuals themselves. Nevertheless, there is as yet, insufficient evidence to suggest with confidence that the level of self-esteem is the most important criterion in assessing educational potential, and consequently of accounting for the relative achievement of different ethnic groups in British society. What seems certain, however, is that positive self-image is essential to achieving success in both educational and occupational life in this modern complex society.

Research Methodology

This chapter draws upon material collected for a large-scale study conducted in British schools. The aim of the study, derived from three linked projects, was to gain an insight into educational, social, cultural and psychological processes which contribute to educational achievement for various ethnic groups in Britain. The subjects were adolescents in the Leeds/Bradford areas of West Yorkshire. The sample of over 1500 consisted of youngsters who were or had completed their last year of compulsory schooling. The research design employed an admixture of quantitative and qualitative techniques; these were used to give the study breadth and depth. The methodological considerations pertaining to research techniques and tools are discussed elsewhere (Verma with Ashworth, 1986).

The youngsters were or had been pupils at nine different schools drawn from two adjacent local authorities. Since the conviction from the outset was that the responses to the last year of compulsory schooling and the various options beyond that stage were likely to be mediated by the differing cultural backgrounds of the youngsters being studied, they were categorized by the ethnic/cultural group, for example, White, Indian, Pakistani, Bangladeshi etc. Such a design facilitated the examination of educational achievement of ethnic minority adolescents, since the data collected offered information on many factors relating to achievement.

One of the tools used in the main study, the concern of this paper, was the fifty-eight item Coopersmith Self-Esteem Inventory (Coopersmith, 1967). This scale covers three areas: self-esteem in the context of the home and the family; self-esteem in school and peer group; and general evaluation of the self. The inventory has been used cross-culturally in American and British studies (Coopersmith, 1967; Bagley, Verma, Mallick and Young, 1979). The inventory has been factor-analyzed in an Australian study (Edgar *et al.*, 1974), and the results supported the notion of global self-esteem, since all of the sub-scales strongly inter-correlated with one another.

The research findings were built on a model that sought to analyze the impact of a wide range of factors — from school, home, peer group and cultural background. The model had a number of underlying assumptions which, it was considered, would offer a more comprehensive picture of the patterns of achievement than hitherto obtained by other studies in the field. The first of these was that educational achievement — whether expressed in terms of public examination success, type of employment obtained or even in terms of personal satisfaction — was the product of a complex interaction of educational, cultural, and familial factors. An index of academic achievement was obtained for each subject by summation over all examination successes using the weightings of 3 (Ordinary level pass at A grade, Ordinary level pass at B and C grades or Certificate of Secondary Education at grade 1) and 1 (other grades of the Certificate of Secondary Education). In the research no attempt was made to compare achievement between ethnic groups; instead each ethnic group within the analysis was sub-divided into 'high' and 'low' achievers by comparison with the median achievement level for that ethnic group. Analysis was then carried out (for each ethnic group separately) to determine those factors which were associated with the distinction between high and low achievement. This analysis is reported fully elsewhere (Verma with Ashworth, 1986).

The Findings as They Relate to Self-Esteem and Achievement

In this research use of the term 'underachievement' was deliberately avoided. Comparisons across ethnic groups were kept to a minimum in respect of achievement scores by utilizing intra-ethnic rather than inter-ethnic analysis. Our concern in this chapter, however, is to examine the self-esteem patterns of South Asian youngsters and the relationship, if any, between self-esteem and educational achievement in them.

The Coopersmith Self-Esteem Inventory (SEI) which was employed throughout the research, yielded measures of self-esteem derived from interactions at home, at school and with peer group, in addition to the general-self component. It was possible therefore to assess the proportion of self-esteem derived from each of the possible sources. The results in terms of the mean percentage are given in table 1.

Analysis of the data revealed that on the whole, South Asian youngsters (particularly Bangladeshi and Indian) derived a greater proportion of the self-esteem from interactions at school as compared with the white group. Interactions within the home were of particular importance for Bangladeshi adolescents. It is interesting to note that irrespective of the self-esteem scores, the proportion of self-esteem derived from each source differed between ethnic groups. However, no statistically significant differences emerged concerning the ethnic groups studied, which implies that the level of self-esteem is not affected by the ethnicity of the individual. A significant sex difference did emerge, however, on the 'general-self' component where females manifested significantly higher self-esteem.

Table 1: Mean Percentage of Total Self-esteem from Sub-scales

SEI	Pakistani N = 75	Bangladeshi N = 45	Indian N = 70
General-self	53.809	53.401	52.998
Social-self-peers	17.377	15.647	17.695
Home-parents	16.072	16.400	16.171
School-academic	12.750	14.552	14.135

Analysis of the self-esteem data showed that South Asian youngsters had higher total self-esteem than their white counterparts. However, in a follow-up study of these youngsters after leaving school (stage 2 of the research) the situation reversed. Self-esteem levels seemed to have been affected by their employment status and whether they had achieved their job aspirations. Analysis also showed that unemployment was highest amongst South Asian youngsters on leaving school than for the white youngsters. The reduction in self-esteem of the South Asians may be attributable, in part, to the effects of unemployment and failure to achieve their vocational aspirations.

Analysis of part of the third stage of the research indicated that although the direct effects of sex, status and ethnicity did not reach any acceptable level of statistical significance, the interactions between the three factors appeared to be interesting. The 'sex x status' interaction occurred because being unemployed had a greater effect on the self-esteem of males than on females. The 'sex x ethnic group' interaction arose because the general self-esteem of South Asians (Pakistanis in particular) was lower than the general self-esteem of white girls, but the reverse was true for boys. The 'status x ethnic group' interaction might have arisen because being unemployed had than on white youngsters. The three-way interaction was a complex combination in which the self-esteem of the various sub-groups was differently affected.

The school-academic component of self-esteem operated somewhat differently. Here the direct effects of status and ethnicity were significant. The former arose because the school-academic self-esteem of sixth formers was significantly higher than those who had left school. The effect of ethnic group arose because of the self-esteem of Indian and Pakistanis was higher than those of the other ethnic groups.

The variables of sex, status or ethnic group had no significant effect on self-esteem derived from the home situation. This may be due to the fact that almost all the youngsters were still living in the parental home. Thus it is less likely that the status of the individual would affect self-esteem from this source. Clearly, status appeared to have no strong effect on the total self-esteem of the adolescents. Although levels of self-esteem were at approximately the same level for those who were employed and those in the sixth form; those who had left school and were unemployed had significantly lower self-esteem.

Measures of self-esteem were found to be significantly related to

Table 2: *Correlation Coefficients: Elements of Self-esteem and Examination Results*

SEI	Pakistani N = 75	Bangladeshi N = 45	Indian N = 77
General-self	.225	.091	.318
Social-self-peers	.279	.065	.228
School-academic	.035	.416	.389
Home-parents	.216	.202	.023

vocational aspirations for Pakistani and Indian youngsters, and not for Bangladeshi. The highest correlations were obtained for the 'school-academic' element of self-esteem.

On the whole the findings of the study suggest that the South Asian groups are able to maintain, or develop, positive self-regard despite their relatively disadvantaged position in British society. They seem to have positive feelings about themselves as individuals and as members of society.

Before examining the relationship between self-esteem and educational achievement it should be recalled that the intra-ethnic analysis was conducted to elicit the factors which were related to achievement. The results of the main study showed that the independent factors account for different amounts of variance for different ethnic groups. Thus in the achievement process certain factors appeared to be important for some ethnic groups but not for others. This suggests that the processes which underlie educational achievement may be culture-dependent. However, our concern in this chapter is to ascertain the relationships between self-esteem components and educational achievement. The patterns of correlation coefficients are presented in table 2.

The results showed that on the whole self-esteem variables were not important factors in educational achievement for pupils of South Asian origin (Pakistani, Bangladeshi and Indian). However, paternal interest in school performance was an important factor for them. This tends to support Gupta's (1977) findings that parents are the major source of motivation to do well in school for those of South Asian backgrounds.

Analysis of the data showed that South Asian youngsters had a significantly more positive attitude towards school education than their white peers. Their motivational position seemed to be centred around a commitment to school and examination success, possibly in the hope of social mobility or more likely to avoid the damaging effect of failure. One possible interpretation of this result is that South

Asian teenagers perceive formal education as a means of social and occupational mobility which has been denied their parents.

A particularly interesting pattern emerged from the data, which was the imbalance in intercultural understanding. Although all those youngsters who participated in the study had spent considerable time in multiethnic schools, the South Asian youngsters had adopted a number of English cultural values, but the white population had failed to understand the characteristics of the other ethnic groups. It was also evident that many of the South Asian youngsters had been affected by growing up in Britain. Although many of them found it difficult to express the feelings arising from being 'caught between two cultures' it was clear that some South Asian youngsters felt somewhat confused about their cultural identity.

Conclusions

The results of the main study clearly indicated that the process of educational achievement may be culture-dependent; factors affecting the achievement of one ethnic group may not necessarily affect the achievement of another group. It may be fallacious, therefore, to attempt to explain the achievement process of a particular ethnic minority group from an understanding of the achievement process of the majority.

Analysis of the data for this chapter showed that self-esteem may be derived from interactions and relationships with the home, the school and peer-groups. It may be argued that self-esteem is a mediatory factor between the immediate environment of the individual and educational achievement.

No significant inter-ethnic differences were found in the levels of self-esteem. However, factors contributing to self-esteem varied in their importance for different ethnic groups. South Asian youngsters, for example, derived most of their self-esteem from family and school sources, although girls tended to have lower self-esteem than boys.

The impact of cultural and immediate family background on the ethnic minority child's (particularly South Asian) values and attitudes to education in general and to school in particular were more marked than those of the white child. The categorization of ethnic minority youngsters into ethnic-cultural groups showed a number of variations from group to group; each group seemed to contain other significant variations because of differing cultural traditions and cultural adaptation to life in Britain. The need for the appreciation and understanding of those potential variations cannot be overstressed. If a climate of increasing inter-ethnic tolerance and understanding is allowed to grow, there would be more chance of ethnic minority adaptation to a new 'cultural' climate which will facilitate freer movement for the youngster between the cultural elements of school, peers and home.

Acknowledgement

The authors are indebted to colleagues Brandon Ashworth and Tony Neasham for their assistance at all stages of the research project on which this chapter is based.

References

BAGLEY, C. (1982) 'Achievement, behaviour disorder and social circumstances in West Indian children and other groups' in VERMA, G.K. and BAGLEY, C. (Eds) *Self-Concept, Achievement and Multicultural Education*, London, Macmillan.

BAGLEY, C., MALLICK, K. and VERMA, G.K. (1979) 'Pupil Self-esteem: A study of black and white teenagers in British schools' in VERMA G.K. and BAGLEY C. (Eds) *Race, Education and Identity*, London, Macmillan.

BAGLEY, C., VERMA, G.K. and MALLICK, K. (1982) 'The comparative structure of self-esteem in British and Indian adolescents' in VERMA G.K. and BAGLEY C. (Eds) *Self-concept, Achievement and Multicultural Education*. London, Macmillan.

BAGLEY, C., VERMA, G.K. MALLICK, K. and YOUNG, L. (1979) *Personality, Self-esteem and Prejudice*, Farnborough, Saxon House.

BROOKS, D. and SINGH, K. (1978) *Aspirations Versus Opportunities: Asian and White School Leavers in the Midlands*, London, Commission for Racial Equality.

COARD, B. (1971) *How the West Indian Child is made Educationally Subnormal by the British Educational System*, London, New Beacon.

COOPERSMITH, S. (1967) *The Antecedents of Self-Esteem*, San Francisco CA, Freeman.

COOPERSMITH, S. (1975) 'Self-concept, race and education' in VERMA, G.K. and BAGLEY, C. (Eds) *Race and Education across Cultures*, London, Heinemann.

DRIVER, G. (1977) 'Cultural competence, social power and school achievement', *New Community*, 5, pp 353–9.

EDGAR, P. *et al.* (1974) *An Analysis of the Coopersmith Self-concept Theory*, California, Goodyear.

GUPTA, Y.P. (1977) 'The educational and vocational aspirations of Asian immigrant and English school-leavers', *British Journal of Sociology*, 28, pp 179–208.

KORMAN, A.K. (1966) 'Self-esteem variable in vocational choice', *Journal of Applied Psychology*, 50, 6, pp 479–86.

LABENNE, W. and GREENE, B. (1969) *Educational Implications of Self-concept Theory*, California, Goodyear.

LOUDEN, D. (1980) 'Self-esteem and locus of control: Some findings on immigrant adolescents in Britain', *New Community*, 6, pp 218–34.

MILNER, D. (1975) *Children and Race*, Harmondsworth, Penguin.

PRENDERGAST, M. and BINDER, D. (1975) 'Relationships of selected self-concept and academic achievement measures', *Measurement and Evaluation Guidance*, 8, pp 92–5.

PURKEY, W.W. (1978) *Inviting School Success: A Self-concept Approach to Teaching and Learning*, Wadsworth Publishing Co. Inc.

SIMON, W. and SIMON, M. (1975) 'Self-esteem, intelligence and standardized academic achievement', *Psychology in the Schools*, 12, pp 97–9.

STONE, M. (1981) *The Education of the Black Child in Britain*, Glasgow, Fontana.

TRIANDIS, H. (1976) 'The future of pluralism', *Journal of Social Issues*, 32, pp 179–208.

VERMA, G.K. (1981) *Problems of Vocational Adaptation of South Asian Adolescents in Britain, with Special Reference to the Role of the School*, unpublished Report, Bradford, University of Bradford.

VERMA, G.K. (1982) 'The problems of vocational adaptation of Asian adolescents in Britain: Some theoretical and methodological issues' in VERMA, G.K. and BAGLEY, C. (Eds) *Achievement and Multicultural Education*, London, Macmillan.

VERMA, G.K. (1983) 'Consciousness, disadvantage and opportunity: the struggle for South Asian youth in British society' in BAGLEY, C. and VERMA G.K. (Eds) *Multicultural Childhood: Education, Ethnicity and Cognitive Styles*, Aldershot, Gower Publishing.

VERMA, G.K. with ASHWORTH, B. (1986) *Ethnicity and Educational Achievement in British Schools*, London, Macmillan.

VERMA, G.K. and BAGLEY, C. (1982) *Self-concept, Achievement and Multicultural Education*, London, Macmillan.

WEIDMAN, H. (1969) 'The self-concept as a crucial link between social science and psychiatric theory', *Transcultural Psychiatric Research*, 6, pp 113–6.

WEINLAND, T., GABLE, R. and VARMING, O. (1976) 'Self-concept: A cross-cultural study', *Perceptual and Motor Skills*, 42, pp 43–6.

12   The Brent Inquiry: Findings and Implications

Jocelyn Barrow

Prior to consideration of the findings and implications of the Brent Inquiry, it is necessary to mention the problems encountered over the availability of the Report. The inquiry had been at the mercy of the differing stances of the local political parties towards it. Successive changes in the character of the political administration in Brent have now brought positive attitudes replacing earlier negative ones to the inquiry and the Report. The present Labour administration in Brent had decided to print the Inquiry Report. This it is hoped will be available shortly. The Brent Report is not as long as the Swann Report (Commitee of Inquiry into the Education of Children from Ethnic Minonty Group 1985) which had covered England and Wales. However, the size of the Brent Report was not inconsiderable, given that it dealt with only *one* local education authority.

Brent's system of education is in a profound crisis. In November 1983, an inquiry was set up to look into the concerns of parents and the standards achieved by pupils attending the Authority's secondary schools. This was because a large number of parents, both black and white, were concerned and vociferous about extremely poor examination results in schools in the Authority. If one is interested in examination results one will find that, over the last four or five years, examination results in the schools in Brent have fallen below the national average. There appeared to be a considerable disparity in examination results between schools in the north and those in the south. The schools in the north enjoyed, it was said, far better facilities and resources than those in the south. Even though examination results in the Borough as a whole were below the national average, those from schools in the northern part were above that average, whereas those from schools in the southern part fell some way below the average.

In November 1983 the Council decided to set up an inquiry to investigate matters. I was asked to lead it and the letter inviting me to conduct it set out the terms of reference. These I will describe in the following pages, since the Report is not yet generally available. I will also bring out some of the background to the inquiry, since I think this is important in understanding the context in which the team set out to do the work.

The terms of reference were: first, to assess the standards achieved in the Authority's fifteen secondary schools; secondly, without moving away from the generality of this objective, to lay emphasis on assessment of the concerns of parents, and in particular black parents, about the levels of provision and achievement and to advise the Council on the justification for such concerns; and thirdly, to report the proceedings and recommendations to the Council and, in particular, to advise on any remedial action needed to improve standards of education.

We were given a year in which to do this work. That was the agreement. It was going to be carried out by a small team. In the end the team consisted of seven members.

Immediately prior to the setting up of the Inquiry, during 1980 and 1981, a system of school appraisals had been instituted after a very long and very difficult period of consultation with the teachers in the area and with the teachers' unions. Under this system, each school in the appraisal system would establish its own goals and objectives and would periodically assess those goals and objectives and, apply a process of self-monitoring. Subsequently, every three years the inspectorate would come in as a team, (actually in Brent they are called advisers). The advisers would go in and, working as a team, would look at the school from their own perspective, that is from the advisers' perspectives. The school would then consider what each group had found out and they would produce an agreed document that was to go to the governors. In other words, each school was asked to monitor itself, having set its own goals. The advisers would visit and see how far those goals had been achieved and an agreed document would be put to the governors of the school.

In spite of such appraisals, parents were still extremely unhappy and therefore the inquiry was set up. There are only fifteen county secondary schools in Brent. It is a very tight and compact area to investigate. We intended to look at each school, not from the self-appraisal point of view, not as a set of advisers, but to establish the perceptions and expectations of the teachers, the parents and the pupils. To do this we intended to set up a series of questionnaires which we would administer in the schools ourselves. We had hoped to work on a school-by-school basis, administering questionnaires to teachers, pupils and their parents. We would then analyze the material we obtained and put it back to the teachers in the hope that this would lead to a meaningful dialogue concerning what was happening in each school. From what emerged in the investigations in each school, we planned to build up a picture of what was happening in the Borough as a whole. However, as things turned out, it was difficult for us to do this. After some initial consultation even before the team had started to work, with the headteachers' representatives, with the Chief Education Officer and her Deputy and getting their agreement to the way in which we intended to work, the teachers' unions, that is the teachers' panels of the Brent Teachers' Association, refused to co-operate. This meant we had to rethink the way in which we were going to work.

We had intended to carry out a school-based inquiry but were unable to gain direct access to the schools. Every member of the research team was a teacher and still active in teaching at a variety of levels. We spent a lot of time trying to get the members of the teachers' unions and the heads to see our point of view. This they found extremely difficult. In the end we realized that, if the work was to go ahead, we would have to think of other ways of working.

We then decided that we would collect all the information on each school centrally, that is, from the local education authority itself. We would get pupils and the parents to complete the questionnaires in their homes. We set up an elaborate system for interviewing parents and pupils and those teachers who were willing to come and talk to us. I want to stress that, in spite of the fact that we did not officially have the cooperation of the teachers' unions, we actually had a very high proportion of teachers, including heads, who cooperated with us and came and met us both as individuals and as groups. In the case of one particular school we had the cooperation of 90 per cent of the school staff. They hired a community hall, because we were not allowed access into the school, to come and meet us and give evidence and answer our questionnaire. There was a great deal of cooperation at an individual and group level. Because we had to get our information in this particular way it meant that it took us a much longer time to do it. It also affected, to some extent, the nature of the information obtained and its generalizability.

One of the things that we discovered was that the local education authority did not have available centrally all the necessary information on each school. This meant we had to establish a procedure by which the local education authority obtained the information we wanted from each school for us. There was not, as in many other local education authorities where I have done research, a central point for obtaining all the information required on schools: infant schools, primary schools, secondary schools, colleges of further education. There was no such centralized bank of information. Therefore we had to set out all the categories of information we wanted and get the local authority to send for it. This presented great difficulties.

We then took evidence from the public in addition to that from the sources already mentioned. We invited written evidence as well as oral evidence and we had a very good response to that. We were able to get what members of the public, other than the actual parents of Brent's secondary school pupils, were saying in addition to the evidence from the advisers, the Chief Education Officer and the deputies, all the top administrative hierarchy of the local education authority and all the chairmen of the local education authority over the last twenty-five years. We considered that we had a good cross-section of information on which to build the report.

Our concern is education for all. We found that a lot of what was said in the Swann Report we would have common ground with. We went much further than Swann in particular respects and in one respect in particular. We discovered that racism was at the heart of a lot of parental complaints, and not just black parents and parents of pupils from other minority ethnic groups, but white parents as well.

The very first piece of written evidence that we received was from a white parent who had been increasingly upset over a very long period because his son had been at school with a young Afro-Caribbean child who was his best friend. From the time they went to school the Afro-Caribbean child had been doing better than his own son. They went through the infant and primary school together, with his son competing quite actively with his best friend but his best friend keeping the lead. As soon as they got into secondary school the divisions began, and the divisions were based on teacher allocations of where the Afro-Caribbean pupil was placed. The point that really upset the parent was the fact that his son was put in for 'O' level and the Afro-Caribbean boy for CSE. That was the first piece of written evidence we received. We would not wish to generalize to the secondary school system as a whole on the basis of one such piece of evidence. The example is used to illustrate the nature of parental concerns. More substantial evidence showed that there was concern about the way in which the schools were being administered and that this was not just from the minority point of view.

A significant portion of the inquiry team's time and of the Report was occupied by a consideration of the ideas and opinions parents hold about their children's education. We were interested in collecting and analyzing their views and finding out why they were held so that we could make a series of recommendations, ensuring that parents' voices could more effectively determine how educational policy could be changed to meet their children's needs. To give the reader an idea of the undertaking we analyzed 1176 questionnaires and conducted about 680 in-depth interviews.

Parents' answers to the questionnaires and opinions expressed at the interviews gave us a clear indication that parents from all ethnic groups were highly dissatisfied with the quality of many aspects of schooling and the implementation of policy by the local authority. Our analysis led us to conclude that a biased school curriculum, poor discipline, poor teacher-pupil relationship, unsatisfactory school and home contacts contributed to a large extent to the failure among Afro-Caribbean and Asian youths to succeed within the educational system.

We found that racism was at the heart of the complaints the parents were making. Additionally, by the very way in which schools were structured, teachers' expectation and teachers' lack of motivation adversely affected the motivation of the minority ethnic group children. That is why racism is one of the largest chapters in the Report. It impinges on a great deal of other things that the Report says, but it is at the heart of the findings.

We were able to link the Brent report with the Swann Report. There were two paragraphs in Swann Report which we thought had particular relevance for the Brent Inquiry and we quoted them in the Report. I will mention both of them. The first one states: 'It will be evident that society is faced with a dual problem: eradicating the discriminatory attitudes of the white majority on the one hand and, on the other, involving an educational system which ensures that all pupils achieve their full potential'. This form of words clothes the problem of racism in the type of language that allowed it to become acceptable and therefore the media did not pick it up. The second statement identifies a problem that is specifically one for the educational system: 'A start has been made in recent years but there is still a long way to go before schools bring out the full potential of all their pupils, and in this context particularly their ethnic minority pupils.' What both of those statements say, is what we have said in the Brent Report in probably a much stronger, more forceful and more direct way about racism.

In looking at Brent, we have called the Report *Two Kingdoms*. It is important to stress that because of reorganization in 1964 of boroughs, Brent was made up of a very affluent north which runs from Sudbury right through to the North Circular Road, and a very poor south which runs from the North Circular back to Kilburn. In taking evidence from one very senior education administrator, he said his perception was that it was almost like two kingdoms: a white, comfortable, affluent (and he did not add Conservative, but in the reality of the politics it is Conservative) north, and a poor, deprived, mainly black, neighbour to the south.

If one compares the results between the schools in the north and the schools in the south of Brent one will see that the south comes out fairly badly. On the whole the borough does badly. If one uses, and we did, the DES Statistical Bulletin of 1982 to compare authorities, Brent, along with three other inner city LEAs, comes into cluster F and thus had — and I quote — 'a substantially above-average score measured in each of the indicators that determine the difficulties and disadvantages in a borough'. We are talking of a borough which, although there is an affluent north and a very poor south, gives the overall impression of an area with all the disadvantages of an inner city, with all the complexities and difficulties which that carries in education.

There is the marked disparity between the quality of the provision in the schools in the north of the Borough and those in the south, and in the resultant performance of their pupils in public examinations.

In very many ways Brent is a microcosm of the entire education system. Much of what the Report says has implications not just for Brent but for very many other local education authorities in the country. It has, as we discovered, special features in addition to those I have just mentioned. We found a situation in which there was a marked isolation between the various areas of education. Professionals in the schools, people in further education, adult and community work, careers service and the youth service were not communicating with one another. It was only when the inquiry was started, and we were taking evidence and talking to a variety of people, did the staff in schools know what the people in adult and community education or even in youth or careers services were doing. There was an isolation between services characterized by very poor communication. Groups were all working within their own prescribed spheres and setting their own goals with no overall policy for the borough as a whole. Another feature characterized the present situation in Brent; there were strong vertical channels of communication but weak lateral channels, and the channels were stronger in passing messages down than passing messages up.

When the inquiry team started work, this was also the mode in which the advisers worked. When we started the study, a chief adviser had just been appointed. As a result of our contact with him which extended over a period of some six to eight days, collecting evidence from him and then seeking his corroboration of the verbatim transcript of his evidence, he was able to appreciate what we meant when we talked about the isolation we had discovered between the various parts of the service. As a result of the interim work report, the LEA began to put that right even before the final report came out.

The other issue that we found from the complaints from parents, was a great lack of confidence in the entire system. There were teachers and pockets of work happening in schools which were very good but overall the total community of Brent had lost confidence in the educational system. This was very unfortunate and was very clearly illustrated by the fact that Brent as a local education authority has one of the highest percentages of children leaving primary school and seeking to continue their education outside the Borough. This appeared common knowledge: teachers knew it, parents knew it, community workers knew it, politicians knew it.

One eminent politician stated that he had been recently to a primary school, and that it was a very good primary school. It was in the south of the Borough. To illustrate how good the school was, there were a large number of councillors' children attending this school although the school was not in their catchment area. The headteacher had said to him 'I will show you something'. He took him into the top class and asked the pupils how many of them were going to secondary schools in the Borough. Nobody put their hand up. How many were going outside? To quote his words 'A forest of hands went up'. When the question was repeated: 'Is anybody going to a school in this Borough?' one child put his hand up very tentatively because he was embarrassed that he could not persuade his parents to let him go to school outside the Borough.

That was in one of the better primary schools attended by children of councillors. The fact that the system was malfunctioning and the fact that although this was a very good primary school, people were choosing to send their children to secondary schools outside the Borough was a clear indication of things having gone seriously wrong.

Although racism was the most intractable of the problems, the problems of communication were extremely important; no communication of a satisfactory nature existed. This weakness we found at all levels. The advisers complained about the communication with the schools. The schools complained. The teachers who spoke to us complained about communication from the 'office', as they called it. The parents complained about the communication with the school. I have already mentioned that each area worked in its own way. Poor communication was a crucial problem.

The question of accountability was yet another concern in which we found weaknesses. In spite of the fact that informally everybody knew all the things that we have been able to put together in the Report — there was evidence of it throughout the system — the views were not coordinated. Had the LEA had its own research department, which every good local education authority should have, if they had had their own information held centrally, they would have been able to find out all the things said in the Report. As this was not the case, the question of accountability became a major issue. One of the recommendations that the Report makes is that the local education authority should fulfil the responsibility that it has both legally, and in other ways, to ensure that the type of education that it is providing is meeting the needs of the pupils in its schools.

As an authority Brent devotes a substantial proportion of its resources on employing teachers. It has one of the best pupil:teacher ratios in the country in the secondary schools. Despite this, the examination results were so poor. We have already outlined some of the things that schools needed to do. One is the employment of black teachers. Other contributors to this book have given reasons for employing black teachers with which I would agree. A policy for recruitment and promotion is needed, not just to teach in black schools, but to teach throughout the borough. Part of what the Report says is that, even in Brent, there are schools that are still all-white. More black teachers are needed because they represent part of our multicultural society. Since we are living in a changing society, all people, of every ethnic group, ought to be represented in the school staff and in the hierarchy at central office.

When we talked to pupils about this, they were terribly concerned about the ethnic group from which a teacher came. We met one very vociferous group of young people who had left school and gone to a college of further education. They said what they needed were teachers with the right attitudes. If a black teacher had the wrong attitude, he or she was just as bad as a white teacher. What they wanted were teachers with the right attitudes, but they agreed that, since it was a multiethnic society, they should have black and white teachers. Thus teacher attitude was something on which pupils themselves laid a great deal of emphasis. Additionally, the group voiced concern with the way in which schools were organized. They pinpointed the lack of care, the lack of concern and an irrelevant curriculum. These were young people who had not achieved anything up to the age of 16 but were now in further education and achieving. They believed that they had not achieved earlier because people had not cared. They were quite explicit on this point. Unfortunately we have not been able to use all the evidence we have taken. I am hoping that we can later put it together, to reflect more clearly than this summary does, some of the views of the pupils.

The Report is extremely critical of the entire educational system having found that Black children are heavily discriminated against by the way the system works and to a certain extent the unconscious ways in which the educational authorities act. However, we also found a will on the part of most officials and those teachers with whom we could make contact to find ways to improve the situation. They seemed to be aware of the shortcomings of the system and more than willing to institute the necessary measures. If there is a problem in Brent, it is not one of individuals, but of the very inadequate structures which do not allow communication and do not permit flexibility and change.

We then went on to look at the government of schools. We felt that there should be more parent governors, that governors need training, that this should be provided, and that it should be a question of cooperation, not of confrontation.

We looked at the reorganization of schools because part of the problem in Brent is that there is a rapid decline in certain areas of school populations. We thought that it would be useful to have two or three sixth form colleges and to use the manpower that was available much more satisfactorily. What one has in Brent is a large number of schools with too many teachers and not enough pupils and in other schools in the same area there are many pupils and not enough teachers. Paradoxically, although the pupil:teacher ratio is good overall, there are pockets where it is very bad.

Finally, we felt that there ought to be a holistic approach to the curriculum. It should be for the school to set out what its curriculum was and then to present that to the governors and to justify the curriculum to the governors. Now that is already a part of the process which should be there. However, that is not the way it is approached. The governors get the final Report; they do not have any say in setting the objectives or being critical of or questioning the objectives before they are set.

The local education authority, since it has become Labour again, has asked us to produce a summary of the Report for parents. They are going to give each parent a copy of the summary because the LEA has adopted the Report. They are going to use it as a blueprint for their way forward. The way we present the summary is by taking the recommendations that we have made and explaining to parents why each recommendation or each group of recommendations was made. The content is presented in a more readable language for parents. The summary was completed by the end of November 1987. The full printed report should be ready soon. People will be able to have an opportunity of reading and discussing it. As was said earlier, it has implications not just for Brent but for very many other local education authorities.

References

BARROW, J. (Chairperson) (1987) *The Two Kingdoms: Standards and Concerns; Parents and Schools*, report of an Independent Investigation into Secondary Schools in Brent, 1981–1984, Brent, London Borough of Brent.
COMMITTEE OF INQUIRY INTO THE EDUCATION OF CHILDREN FROM ETHNIC MINORITY GROUPS (1985) *Education for All*, (Swann Report) Cmnd. 9453, London, HMSO.

Notes On Contributors

Jocelyn Barrow, OBE is an Honorary Lecturer at the Institute of Education, University of London. She was Chairperson of the Brent Inquiry.

Ann Dawson is an Honorary Research Fellow at the University of Manchester, Department of Education.

Martin Desforges is an Educational Psychologist with the Sheffield Education Department Psychological Service.

Graham Dunn is a Research Officer with the Medical Research Council Child Psychiatry Unit at the Institute of Psychiatry, London.

Tony Kerr is an Educational Psychologist with the Harrow Education Department Psychological Service.

Nicholas J. Mackintosh is Professor of Experimental Psychology in the Department of Experimental Psychology, University of Cambridge.

Kanka Mallick is Senior Lecturer in the Psychology of Education at the West London Institute of Higher Education.

C.G.N. Mascie-Taylor is a Lecturer in the Department of Physical Anthropology, University of Cambridge.

Barbara Maughan is a Senior Research Officer with the Medical Research Council Child Psychiatry Unit at the Institute of Psychiatry, London.

Peter Newsam is Chairman of the Commission for Racial Equality.

Bhikhu Parekh is Professor of Political History at the University of Hull and Deputy Chairman of the Commission for Racial Equality.

Peter Pumfrey is Reader in Education in the Department of Education, University of Manchester.

John Roberts is a Senior Educational Psychologist working for the Warwickshire School Psychological Service.

Gejendra Verma is Reader in Education and Director of the Centre for Ethnic Studies in Education in the Department of Education, University of Manchester.

A.M. West is a Research Student at the Department of Experimental Psychology, University of Cambridge.

Index